CHOICES & CONSE= QUENCES

WHAT TO DO WHEN A TEENAGER USES ALCOHOL/DRUGS

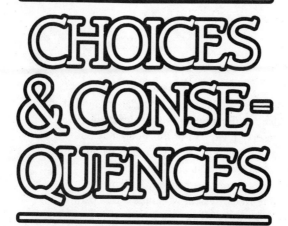

CHOICES & CONSE= QUENCES

WHAT TO DO WHEN A TEENAGER USES ALCOHOL/DRUGS

A STEP-BY-STEP SYSTEM THAT *REALLY WORKS*

By Dick Schaefer
Edited by Pamela Espeland

JOHNSON INSTITUTE

HAZELDEN·

Hazelden Information and Educational Services
Center City, Minnesota 55012-0176
1-800-328-9000 (Toll Free U.S., Canada, and the Virgin Islands)
1-651-213-4000 (Outside the U.S. and Canada)
1-651-213-4590 (24-hour Fax)
www.hazelden.org

Library of Congress Cataloging-in-Publication Data
Schaefer, Dick
Choices & consequences.

 Bibliography: p.
 1. Youth--United States--Alcohol use. 2. Alcoholism--
United States--Prevention. 3. Youth--United States--
Drug Use. 4. Drug abuse--United States--Prevention.
I. Espeland, Pamela, 1951-   . II. Title. III Title:
Choices & consequences.
HV5135.S33   1987   362.2'9   87-22717
ISBN 0-935908-42-0

PRINTED IN THE UNITED STATES OF AMERICA

11 10 9

Dedication

This book is dedicated to the outreach workers — Connie, Marty, Willie, Sandi, Shelley, Leigh, Kim, John, Sheila, Kisa, and Lynde — who are the "cookie people" for many teenagers in trouble with alcohol/drugs, and to Bev and Bob and parents everywhere in self-help groups who give hope to families that miracles are still possible.

Acknowledgments

First there is Mary, my wife and companion, who stood by me during the writing of this book — giving me support, feedback, and constant encouragement.

Then there are my friends across the country — Tom Alibrandi, Ross Ramsey, John Horsey, Betty Anderson, and Craig Bader — who have shared generously with me over the years their insights in working with teenagers, many of which have found their way into this book.

Also there are my friends and colleagues in our local network system — Patrick Curran, Mark Haugen, Jim Thom, Jim Shipp, Jane Kihl-Kippley, and Mark Stutrud — who while working in the trenches with teenagers and their parents still found time to share their thoughts and ideas about the procedures described in this book.

Finally there is Carole Remboldt of the Johnson Institute, who made this book possible with her invitation to write it, her honest criticisms, and her never-ending support. And Pamela Espeland, who patiently worked with us to edit and revise the manuscript. I am deeply indebted to both of them for sharing their skills and insights.

Contents

Part II: Intervening with Teenagers in Trouble with Alcohol/Drugs

Part III: Resources

A Few Words About "Alcohol/Drugs"

You'll notice the term "alcohol/drugs" in the title of this book and in many places throughout it.

We use it to emphasize that alcohol is a drug — just like cocaine, marijuana, uppers, downers, or any other mood-altering substance.

Too often people talk about "alcohol or drugs" or "alcohol and drugs" as if alcohol is somehow different from drugs and in a category by itself. Our culture, our government, even our laws treat alcohol differently than they treat so-called "other drugs" like pot, crack, smack, and so on down the list.

But the symptoms of dependence are essentially the same, and the need for intervention is just as urgent.

Preface

My work in chemical dependence began in 1966 as a chaplain at the Heartview Foundation Treatment Center for Alcoholism in Mandan, North Dakota. It was there that I met Vernon Johnson at his first North Dakota training session on the process of intervention.

At that time, most people in treatment were adults. During the late 1960s we had only two or three teenagers a year come in for treatment — and we treated them like adults.

Since 1970, I have worked full time with teenage alcohol/ drug users — in an inpatient setting at the State Hospital, in an outpatient program at a mental health center, and with an outreach program in schools and communities. I have learned that while intervention works with teenagers, the process must be different from the one used with adults. At the Touch Love Center in Fargo, we treat teenagers like teenagers. And we are rewarded again and again with success.

The system described in this book works. We see the proof every day. And I am confident that you will, too, as you begin the difficult task of trying to help *your* teenager.

Dick Schaefer
Fargo, North Dakota
February, 1996

Introduction

Every parent of a teenager today worries about drugs. Every teacher knows that some of his or her students are experimenting with them. Every family doctor, pediatrician, and school nurse must be alert to the signs of alcohol and other drug use. Every mental health professional, social services worker, juvenile justice worker, and clergy youth worker must be prepared to deal with chemical use among the young people he or she sees.

If you're a parent, a teacher, or anyone else who spends time with teenagers in your professional or personal life, you have good reason to be deeply concerned about alcohol and other drugs.

We know that drugs continue to cause premature deaths in this country. Joseph A. Califano, Jr., Director of the Center for Addiction and Substance Abuse (CASA), reports that alcohol abuse kills more than 100,000 Americans each year, and illegal drug use claims at least 20,000 lives.[1]

In the last few years, there has been an increase in the use of drugs among students in school. Through a survey funded by the National Institute on Drug Abuse (NIDA), the Institute for Social Research at the University of Michigan has been monitoring drug use of students for more than twenty-one years. From 1979 to 1991, the use of illicit drugs actually decreased. Since 1992, however, there has been an alarming increase in the use of all illicit drugs.

- The 1994 National Household Survey showed that marijuana use has almost doubled among 12 to 17 year-olds in two years — from 4.0% to 7.3%. This amounts to 1.3 million adolescents. In the same 12 to 17 year-old age group:
  - 1.8 million adolescents used illicit drugs.
  - 11 million adolescents drank alcohol regularly.

- 2 million adolescents drank heavily, consuming 5 or more drinks at least five times a month.
- 4 million adolescents smoked cigarettes in an average month.[2]
• The 1995 Survey conducted by PRIDE (National Parents' Resource Institute for Drug Education) of 200,000 students revealed that one in ten junior high students smoked marijuana during the 1994-95 school year. The study further found that during this time:
  - Beer drinking was at a 5-year high for high school students and at a 2-year high for junior high students.
  - 20% of 6th graders drank beer or wine coolers at least once in 1995.[3]
• The 1995 University of Michigan's NIDA survey of 50,000 students reported that illicit drug use doubled from 1991 to 1995 for 8th graders (11% to 21%). Since 1992 the 10th graders increased their use from 20% to 33%. and the 12th graders' use of illicit drugs jumped from 27% to 39%.

  Marjiuana use has the highest increase since 1991 for any drug use reported during 1995: 8th graders — from 6% to 16%; 10th graders — from 15% to 29%; and 12th graders — from 22% to 35%.

  Other drugs, such as LSD, speed, cocaine, heroin, inhalants, and nicotine increased in usage during this same period of time.

  Alcohol use among students also increased somewhat during this period of time, but it still remains at the highest level of all drugs. For students drinking at the abuse level (5 or more drinks at one sitting) the survey showed: 8th graders at 15%; 10th graders at 24%; and 12th graders at 30%.[4]
• The 1995 *StudentView®* Survey of the Johnson Institute showed similar results for students drinking alcohol at problem use levels. The survey reported: 8th graders at 15.4%; 10th graders at 31%; and 12th graders at 34%. In

addition, this same survey revealed the following percent-
ages of adolescents for being at risk for chemical dependence: 8th graders at 2.5%; 10th graders at 7.2%; and 12th
graders at 10%.[5]

These are the hard, cold facts about alcohol and other drug
use among teenagers. Any adult who cares about kids can't
help but be profoundly disturbed about these numbers and
their implications.

Why is this so? What is going on here? These are concerns
of all of us who care about our teenagers. Dr. Lee Brown,
Director of the Office of National Drug Control Policy, states
that "the increase in the first-time use of marijuana by young-
sters 12 to 17 years old should serve as a profound wake-up
call to parents...it makes me fear for the future of our children
if we do not take effective action now."[6] Dr. Lloyd Johnston,
who conducts the NIDA survey at the University of
Michigan, suggests that the increase in drug use since 1992
may reflect a "generational replacement process." Younger
kids just don't know what their older brothers and sisters
knew about drugs. It's like they are going through the 70s all
over again. Dr. Johnston calls this "generational forgetting."[7]

There are several reasons for this "generational forgetting."
For one thing, less information is getting out to teenagers
alerting them about the dangers of drug use. And there has
been increasing encouragement from the media for young
people to use alcohol and other drugs. Through television,
movies, and advertising campaigns, both the alcohol and
tobacco industries seem to have targeted kids. In addition, the
popular music of today — rap, grunge, and heavy metal —
seems to celebrate the effects of drugs, and therefore, further
desensitizes young people's perception of the risks and haz-
ards of drug use.

Results of recent surveys support the reality of the desensi-
tization of young people to the risks inherent in the use of

alcohol and other drugs. The 1995 *Weekly Reader* Survey of 25,000 elementary school students report that 21% of children in grades 4 through 6 do not think wine coolers are dangerous; 17% do not see any danger in sniffing glue; and 49% do not think smoking can be harmful.[8] The *1994 Household Survey* revealed that only 42% of 12 to 17 year-old teenagers think pot is harmful.[9] And statistics from the 1995 NIDA Survey from the University of Michigan showed that at the 8th grade level only 50% think there is a risk involved in smoking more than a pack of cigarettes a day.[10]

In addition to the rising incidence of alcohol and other drug use among adolescents, it is worth noting that a significant number of treatment centers and drug rehabilitation centers have closed in recent years.So it is that at a time when there clearly is a need for *more* inpatient treatment programs, we are seeing them decline at an accelerated rate, due — in large part — to increasing costs and the lack of insurance coverage. A growing number of outpatient centers are developing intensive programs in an effort to fill the gap created by the closing of inpatient treatment centers. These centers, however, cannot keep up with the demand for services, nor can they replace the methods that inpatient care offers.

Despite the bad news about declining services from inpatient treatment facilities, there is some good news on the horizon: educational programs and detention centers can and do help many kids with their alcohol and other drug use problems. And there is much that can be done — through public awareness campaigns and concerted efforts to educate and sensitize our kids — to to change the way we accept the widespread use of these substances.

But the best news of all is this: *you can do something*. If you're a parent who thinks that your teenager may be using, *you can do something*. If you're a teacher who suspects that some of your students are coming to class drunk or high, *you can do something*. If you're a guidance counselor, a coach, a family physician, a neighbor, or a friend who cares, *you can do something.*

This book describes what you can do to help a teenager who is using alcohol or other drugs. It describes a process called *intervention* that has been proven effective for over 30 years. It tells you precisely how to use this process to stop a teenager's harmful involvement with chemicals and start him or her on the road to a richer, fuller, healthier life.

The intervention process as presented here involves a structured series of choices and consequences — choices made available to the teenager, and consequences that result from those choices. As an adult, you wield considerable influence over the teenagers in your home or classroom. But one thing you *can't* do is simply order them to stop using alcohol or other drugs and expect them to obey. Nor can you instruct them to "just say no" and leave it at that.

Instead, you can make using alcohol and other drugs increasingly undesirable, and not using these substances increasingly desirable. By making it clear that continued use will lead to certain fixed and inflexible outcomes, you can help a teenager *want* and *choose* to stop using. And that, of course, is the key.

Notes

1. Joseph A. Califano, "Legalization: The Reality," *The Prevention Pipeline,* Center for Substance Abuse Prevention (September 10, 1995) pp. 11-12.

2. *National Household Survey on Drug Abuse:* 1994, Rockville, MD: SAMHSA Office of Applied Studies (September 12, 1995).

3. PRIDE Release, *Annual Survey on Drug Use,* Atlanta: PRIDE (November 2, 1995).

4. NIDA, "National High School Survey," Ann Arbor, MI: University of Michigan Survey Research Center (December 11, 1995).

5. *StudentView® Survey Report,* From January 1, 1994 to August 31, 1995. Minneapolis: Johnson Institute (December 1, 1995).

6. Lee Brown, "Marijuana Use By Teens—On the Rise," *The Prevention Pipe-line,* Center for Substance Abuse Prevention (September/October, 1995) p. 8.

7. Lloyd D. Johnston, "National High School Survey," Ann Arbor, MI: University of Michigan Survey Research Center (December 11, 1995) p. 6.

8. *The Weekly Reader National Survey on Drugs, Alcohol, and Tobacco, Middleton,* CT: Weekly Reader Company, 1995.

9. *National Household Survey on Drug Abuse: 1994.* Rockville, MD: SAMHSA Office of Applied Studies (September 12, 1995).

10. NIDA, "National High School Survey," Ann Arbor, MI: University of Michigan Survey Research Center (December 11, 1995).

CHAPTER

1

"You Sat on the Burner, Baby. . .You Sit on the Blisters" and Other Basic Principles of Intervention

You have reason to believe that a teenager you know — your son or daughter, a student, an employee or a friend — is using alcohol/drugs. You think you should do something because you feel responsible for him or her.

Wrong! You are not responsible *for* others, but *to* them. This is the first basic principle of intervention. Believing it will free you to exercise your responsibility in ways that work.

- "You are not responsible for others" means that you cannot control another person's behavior, feelings, or decisions.
- "You are responsible to others" means that you can control these two things: yourself, and your environment.

You can control your own behavior toward, feelings about, and decisions concerning others. You can control the environment that is under your care — the home, the school, or wherever else you come into contact with teenagers as a person in authority.

This principle is easier to understand if we apply it to our interactions with little children. Picture, for example, a scene we've all witnessed more than once: a grocery store, a set of parents, and a three-year-old throwing a temper tantrum.

How do parents handle this situation? Some shout at the child. Some threaten the child. Some buy the child anything he or she wants, just to get a few moments of peace and quiet. Some hit the child.

In other words, the parents try to control the child's behavior. A far better approach is to ignore the child's behavior and control their own by not shouting, threatening, giving in, or hitting. If this doesn't get results, they can move on to controlling the environment: They can take the child out of the store.

That makes sense, you say. But what about the teenager who comes in two hours late, obviously intoxicated, loud and argumentative? (And he — or she — drove your car home!) Some behaviors can't be ignored. How do you control the environment? Do you remove the teenager from the premises, or is that even the thing to do? Do you yell and accuse and complain? Or do you look the other way, telling yourself that "kids will be kids"?

Now we're talking about the need for a whole new strategy, *but the principle is the same*. You can't control your teenager's behavior. You can't control his or her feelings. You can't make his or her decisions. But you *can* control how you yourself react to the situation, and you *can* control the environment to set the stage for positive change.

When you try to control the behavior of someone who uses alcohol/drugs, you become what chemical dependence professionals call an *enabler*. Enablers are people — usually family or friends — who take responsibility for the behaviors, feelings, and decisions of the user. Out of love, concern, fear, or a combination of these, they react and behave in ways that shield the user from experiencing the consequences of his or her alcohol/drug use. They mean well, but *the effect of their actions is to make it easier for the user to keep using*.

Let's look at some examples of enabling behaviors. We'll take the scenario of the teenager (a boy, for the sake of convenience) coming home drunk. He stumbles into the house, where Mom and Dad are anxiously waiting.

Dad says: "You're drunk!" *(Accusing behavior.)* "You know our rules about drinking alcohol. You are NOT allowed to drink, and that's that!" *(Laying-down-the-law behavior.)*

Mom says: "What's wrong with you? You know better than to drink and drive! Have you lost every bit of common sense?" *(Provoking behavior.)* "I'll bet it's those friends you've been hanging around with; I knew they were no good!" *(Laying-the-blame elsewhere behavior.)*

Dad says: "It had better not happen again, or else!" *(Threatening behavior.)*

Mom says: "How could you do this to us? Don't you know how much we love you, and how hard we've worked to give you a good home?" *(Guilt-inducing behavior.)*

Dad says: (to Mom and himself): "I'm at my wits' end with this kid. If it isn't one thing, it's another. He never listens to us anymore." *(Feelings-of-helplessness behavior.)*

Mom says: "I can see that this conversation isn't doing any of us any good. And Frank" (the son) "looks terrible. Maybe this isn't the time to talk. Honey, why don't you go get ready for bed, and I'll come and tuck you in?" *(Caretaking behavior.)*

Dad (grumbling) says: "And I'll go make sure the car is in the garage." *(Taking-responsibility-for behavior.)*

Both say: "Well, I guess it's no big deal. . .after all, boys will be boys." *(Making-excuses-for behavior.)*

What's happened here? The parents have let their son off the hook. They have helped him to avoid the consequences of his behavior. They have taken those consequences upon themselves and *enabled* him to keep using.

Intervention demands that one stop enabling (being responsible for) and start really caring (being responsible to). This is the first thing we teach people who live with alcohol/ drug abusers: *Stop trying to control them.*

My Aunt Liz, who died at age 93, had a saying she used when I was going through some tough times as a teenager: "You sat on the burner, baby...you sit on the blisters." What she meant was, "You made your choices...now you take the consequences." She never said, "Here, let me suffer for you; let *me* sit on your blisters. She was too smart for that!

Who sits on the blisters of the three-year-old throwing the tantrum in the frozen-foods aisle? The parents who shout, hit, or hand over the candy bar. Who sits on the blisters of the teenager who comes in drunk at 2 a.m.? The parents who yell, accuse, and complain or dismiss the whole thing as "normal teenage behavior" or "sowing wild oats."

Teenagers who use alcohol/drugs are pros at getting others to sit on their blisters. Every time adults react to their behaviors by showing anger, guilt, or hurt feelings, the adults are sitting on their blisters. And if others are willing to experience their pain, why should they change?

The second basic principle of intervention concerns the need for a "connector" — a significant other big person outside of the immediate family whom the teenager can trust and relate to. This person is called the "connector" because he or she "connects" with the teenager through unconditional acceptance.

He or she cares for the teenager *no matter what*, and there are no strings attached to that caring. (Another name for the connector is the "cookie person" — someone who gives you chocolate-chip cookies without reminding you to brush your teeth.) Everyone needs a connector; everyone needs the experience of being accepted unconditionally. Parents can't play this role because it's very difficult to do that *and* fulfill one's responsibilities as parents as well.

So who can? That's a hard question nowadays. Prior to World War II, America was full of extended families. It was not uncommon to find grandparents, parents, aunts and uncles living under the same roof. Some of them were natural "connectors" or "cookie people." In most families today, however, both parents work or one parent is absent and the other relatives live somewhere else — across town or across the country. In 1980, one out of five children lived in single-parent families, and 23 percent of all households were run by single parents.[1] Experts predict that by the early 1990s, some 50 percent of our children will have a single-parent family experience by the time they are 18.[2]

We parents need help! It's difficult to raise our children by ourselves. It's difficult to love them unconditionally while at the same time making and enforcing the rules that will help them to grow into decent, responsible people. We need to find the "connectors" in their lives. Start thinking now about some possible "connectors" in the lives of the teenager(s) you know.

The third basic principal of intervention has to do with the need for a *network* of people willing and able to confront the teenager about his or her alcohol/drug use. No one should attempt such a confrontation alone.

Chemical dependence has been called a "system illness." The chemically dependent teenager is trapped within a *delusional system* supported by many people. We'll talk more about that later; the point to be made here is that *it takes a system to crack a system.*

Successful intervention consists of people working together

to confront the teenager on his or her delusional system. They must present a united front. Teenagers in trouble always manage to find the weakest link — whether at home (parent against parent), at school (teachers against teachers or administrators), or in the community (courts against treatment programs or the schools). They always find a way to slip between the cracks.

If we really want to do something about adolescent alcohol/drug use, we adults must work together. We need one another. And it can be very comforting to realize that, in fact, we have one another. Often all we have to do is put out the word.

Parents, you are not alone! You have the schools and the courts and counselors and treatment centers, ready and willing to help you.

Professionals, you are not alone! You will find allies in the schools and the courts and the homes of troubled teenagers. The network you help to form must be like a brick wall — consistent and unyielding. The teenager must hear the same message from all of you: "You are responsible for your own behaviors and feelings and decisions."

You sat on the burner, baby. . .you sit on the blisters.

Intervention requires us to connect and confront together. Intervention requires us to let teenagers experience the consequences of their own choices.

Remember: you are not responsible *for* the teenager who is using alcohol/drugs. But you can be responsible *to* him or her, and make a very real difference in his or her life.

Notes

1. Census Bureau Current Population Survey, U.S. Bureau of the Census, "Marital Status and Living Arrangements, March 1980," *Current Population Reports,* Series P-30, No. 365 (1981).

2. Dr. Frank Furstenberg, University of Pennsylvania sociologist, quoted in Ellen McCoy, "Kids & Divorce," *Parents Magazine* (November 1984).

Part I

LEARNING ABOUT TEENAGE CHEMICAL DEPENDENCE

Why do teenagers use alcohol/drugs? What causes them to ignore their parents' warnings, disregard what they learn in school and from the media, and decide that they're somehow invulnerable to getting hooked?

And what happens when a teenager starts using? What are the signs that he or she is in trouble? We now know that chemical dependence is a disease with certain describable characteristics. We also know that it proceeds according to clear and definable stages — and that *it can be treated and arrested.*

We know, too, that chemical dependence in teenagers differs from chemical dependence in adults. This is especially important for professional caregivers experienced in working with adults to recognize. What are considered symptoms of chemical dependence in adults can be nothing more than common "adolescent behaviors" in some teens.

There are two things to consider when working with a teenager who is using alcohol/drugs: how far the usage has progressed, and how deeply entrenched the individual is in the adolescent delusional system. What you learn about each will determine how you approach intervention and what kind of intervention you do.

CHAPTER
2

Why Teenagers Use Alcohol/Drugs

One of the first questions parents ask when faced with the fact that a teenager is using alcohol/drugs is, "WHY?"

Why was my son picked up for drunk driving? He knows better! Why did I find a bag of marijuana in my daughter's dresser drawer? She knows better! *Why* is my smart, with-it child doing this dumb and scary thing? Or, why is my difficult and troubled child making his or her life *more* difficult and troubled by using alcohol/drugs?

There are countless reasons why a teenager chooses to use, including low self-esteem, peer pressure, curiosity, escape, excitement, and rebellion. But most can be traced back to external pressures. The real reason *isn't* because teenagers today are all that different than teenagers of 30, 20, or even 10 years ago. We complain about "kids today" as if the world were literally "going to pot," but teenagers have been teenagers since time began.

Four hundred years before Christ, Socrates observed that the youth of his day didn't show respect to their elders, the way *he* did when he was growing up. He complained that they didn't stand up when adults walked into the room, that they spoke before being spoken to, and that they sometimes used foul language.

Our parents complained about us in turn. We didn't work hard enough. . .we spent too much time listening to the radio. . .and on and on. And we complain about our children: they're lazy, they watch too much TV, they dress funny.

Even teenagers themselves complain about their younger siblings — "they have it easy," "they have it good," "how come they get to do things you never let ME do?" And so it goes, from one generation to the next.

Teenagers *per se* haven't changed, but the pressures on them certainly have. They're urged to grow up faster and make important life decisions sooner. And they're encouraged to use chemicals — by their peers and by the culture.

The pressure to use alcohol/drugs has never been stronger than it is now. We talk about the 60s as the decade of free love and "turning on," and the 70s as the "me first" decade, but I believe that the decades of the 80s and 90s have the 60s and the 70s beat. There are four reasons for this:

1. We live in an instant-gratification society with instant-gratification expectations.

The microchip has revolutionized our world. Ask the average teenager if he (or she) has ever used a slide rule. Many haven't even heard of it. When told that we used to multiply, divide, and calculate square roots with a piece of wood and a slider, today's teen will touch buttons on a calculator.

Quite a few years ago, *Time* magazine named the computer its Man of the Year. Most grade-school children know more about computers than the average parent. Add in microwave ovens, instant cameras, and video games, and you start to understand why the notion that "relief is just a pill (or a drink, or a drag) away" holds so much appeal for our youth.

Our pushbutton society has produced a generation of young people who expect things to happen *now,* without having to work for them. The lesson, "Things that count take time," often isn't learned — whether it applies to relationships, working through grief, developing skills, or processing the normal painful feelings of adolescence.

Alcohol/drugs work instantly. All you have to do is get

them into your body and your feelings change in no time, with no real effort on your part.

2. The amount of advertising for alcohol and other drugs has more than doubled within the past fifteen years.

The liquor industry alone has spent billions of dollars to convince you and me and our kids that we can become anything we want to be — sexy, independent, friendly, attractive, strong, successful — by drinking something alcoholic.

And the tobacco industry has spent over $6 billion trying to win over new consumers to replace the 3,000 persons who either quit smoking or die each day.

Count the TV ads for over-the-counter drugs that air on any given evening. Better yet, count the ads in our weekly magazines and on our billboards. Young people are continually bombarded with the message that alcohol/drugs are the answer to all of their questions, the solution to all of their problems and insecurities.

3. The amount of time teenagers spend watching TV has produced an essentially passive generation.

The average high-school senior has watched from 18 to 20 *thousand* hours or television — nearly twice as much time as it takes to graduate from high school.

Too much TV squashes creativity and promotes passivity — a setup for chemical abuse. When you take alcohol/drugs, all you have to do is "let it happen to you." Like watching TV, taking alcohol/drugs is a passive, "do-it-to-me" pursuit.

4. Alcohol/drugs are available in *all* of our communities.

Urban or rural, the statistics are about the same. Interestingly, alcohol — the #1 drug of abuse among adults — is also the #1 drug of abuse among teenagers.

We're a nation at war against illegal drugs — cocaine, heroin, marijuana. Anyone who has read a newspaper or watched the news on TV in recent months is aware of the massive federal effort that has been launched to publicize their dangers and make it harder to buy and sell them.

Unfortunately, we're not making the same effort where alcohol is concerned. Ten years ago, Dr. Otis Bowen, then Secretary of Health and Human Services, pointed out, "Our experience with the consequences of alcohol abuse in America is greater, by far, than our experience with any other drug. Yet I really don't believe we've reached the point where public concern over the extent of our problems and public pressure to prevent and treat them rival that of other major illnesses or the abuse of other drugs.

"The fact is," Dr. Bowen went on to say, "people still don't know all they should. Many don't know just how extensive alcohol abuse and alcoholism are... More people need to know, for example, that...the U.S. ranks sixth in the world in deaths due to alcoholism... More people need to know that nearly 5 million adolescents, or 3 out of every 10, have problems with alcohol.[1]

Donna E. Shalala, the U.S. Department of Health and Human Services present Secretary, agrees with this assessment. She has observed that "...nearly one of every four Americans is directly affected by alcohol or other drug dependency of a family member or friend."[2]

We parents felt relieved in the 70s and 80s when our children were "only" getting drunk. This attitude is still prevalent today, and it keeps us from recognizing and responding to the danger signs of addiction.

Notes

1. *The Alcoholism Report,* Vol. 2, No. 16 (June 9, 1987), p.1
2. Donna E. Shalala, *HHS News,* Rockville, MD: SAMHSA Press Office (Sept. 12, 1995), p. 2

CHAPTER

3

The Addiction Process

It used to be believed that chemical dependence was a sign of low self-control, lax morals, irresponsibility, or some other character flaw or shortcoming. Chemically dependent people were ordered to shape up and get it together, or they were dismissed as "weak-willed" or "just that way."

We know better today. We have substantial evidence that chemical dependence is a disease.

In fact, "The American Medical Association, American Psychiatric Association, American Public Health Association, American Hospital Association, American Psychological Association, National Association of Social Workers, World Health Organization, and the American College of Physicians have now each and all officially pronounced alcoholism as a disease."[1]

In April of 1987, the American Medical Society on Alcoholism and Other Drug Dependencies — whose membership includes over 2,000 M.D.s certified as specialists in chemical dependence — officially declared that *what is true for alcoholism is also true for addiction to other drugs*. According to AMSAODD president Dr. Max Schneider, dependence on drugs other than alcohol "comprises a process similar to alcoholism. . . .The time has now come for the medical profession and society as a whole to look clinically and dispassionately at the entire constellation of these conditions as disease states."[2]

It is important for you to understand and accept this concept. It will go a long way toward relieving your guilt if and when your teenager or another you know is diagnosed as addicted to alcohol/drugs.

No one is to blame for another person's chemical dependence. If a teenager in your home or classroom or care is chemically dependent, you didn't cause it. Furthermore, you can't control it, and you can't cure it.

What a relief it is to admit and accept this! When you stop blaming yourself, you can start letting go of being responsible for your children and start being responsible to them.

What exactly causes addiction? We don't know the answer yet, although there are many theories. For example, the work of Drs. Donald Goodwin, Marc Schuckit, George Winokur, and others has shown that some children seem genetically predisposed to alcoholism — especially those whose biological parents or grandparents are alcoholic.

What we do know is how to tell if someone has this disease. *His or her relationship with the chemical becomes more important than anything else in his or her life.*

Chemical dependence is a "love affair" with the drug of choice. Using drugs becomes more important than relationships, doing well at school or work, planning for the future, or anything else. There's a saying that "chemicals are people substitutes." It's more accurate to say that chemicals are *life* substitutes. Using becomes the reason to get up in the morning and go out at night; it's the be-all and end-all.

Like any other disease, chemical dependence has certain describable characteristics.

1. Chemical dependence is a compulsive, obsessive disease.

We can picture it in terms of a valley chart, with non-addictive usage on the left and addiction on the right.

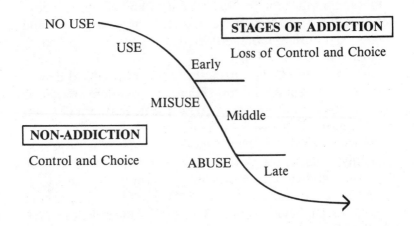

It is possible to distinguish three different levels of involvement on the non-addiction side: use, misuse, and abuse.

- **Use** can be defined as using a chemical to enhance an already pleasurable event — drinking wine at a meal or in a liturgical setting, having a beer at the lake or a cocktail before dinner.
- **Misuse** means that the chemical has occasionally begun to interfere with one or more areas of a person's life. For example, you get drunk on your wedding anniversary when you had no intention of doing so.
- **Abuse** indicates that the chemical has consistently begun to interfere with one or more areas of a person's life. For example, you get drunk with some regularity on weekends. Or you are stopped by the police for driving while intoxicated.

As long as one's use of chemicals stays to the left of the chart, one can still exercise choice about it and control over it. During the addiction process, however, one steadily loses the options of choice and control. It's like having the flu. The addict can no more get up in the morning and say, "I'm going to quit using drugs today," then the person with the flu can say, "I think I'll get well at noon."

For the addict, using alcohol/drugs is a compulsion. Compulsion is a primary symptom of the disease of chemical dependence. It appears to reside within the old "primitive brain" — the hypothalamic instinctual brain — that houses our strongest instincts: to flee or fight, to eat and drink, to reproduce. For the addict, the compulsion to use chemicals is stronger than all five of these instincts combined.

Along with compulsion, there is also an obsession with chemicals. Concerns about "where can I get some," "how much should I get," "who can I trust to buy from and use with," "where should I hide my supply," and so on dominate one's thinking. Chemicals become central to one's life.

2. Chemical dependence is a primary disease.

Once a person embarks on a "love affair" with a chemical, the chemical becomes more important than anything else. The person has a primary relationship with the chemical.

Calling the disease "primary" also means that it's not just a symptom of some other underlying physical or emotional disorder. Instead, it *causes* many such disorders.

This means that other problems a chemical dependent may have — such as physical illness, disturbed family relationships, depression, unresolved grief issues, and trouble at school or on the job — cannot be treated effectively until the person stops using chemicals. The dependence must be treated first.

3. Chemical dependence is a progressive disease.

Once a person enters the addiction process, the disease follows a predictable, progressive course of symptoms. Left untreated, it *always* gets worse.

The normal progression goes from using chemicals with few consequences to using chemicals with greater and more serious consequences, including physical, mental, emotional, and spiritual deterioration.

4. Chemical dependence is a chronic disease.

Once a person is addicted to chemicals, the symptoms of the disease become chronic. This means that he or she can never safely use chemicals again.

As the saying goes, the alcoholic is always "one drink away from a drunk." There is no cure for this condition. In this respect, chemical dependence is similar to diabetes, another chronic disease. In both cases, the victim can have a healthy, happy, and productive life *as long as he or she accepts the need for abstinence.*

For the chemically dependent person, this means *no* use of mood-altering chemicals. As people in treatment centers say, "The disease is called alcoholism, not alcohol*wasm.*"

It used to be believed that chemical dependence was a "learned" behavior and could be "unlearned." Not true. Even after five, ten, fifteen or more years of sobriety, alcoholics who start drinking again usually begin to drink at the same level at which they left off. It doesn't matter how much intellectual understanding they have acquired about the disease, or how firmly they have resolved to stay off alcohol; once they take that first drink, they will take another and another.

Chemical dependence is a lifelong, permanent disease. It

never goes away; it cannot be cured. It can only be arrested. That's why people who get help and quit using are often called "recovering" and not "recovered."

5. Chemical dependence is a fatal disease.

A chemically dependent person usually dies prematurely if he or she continues to use alcohol/drugs. We are not talking about a bad habit; we are talking about life and death!

The average lifespan of an alcoholic is 10 to 12 years shorter than that of a non-alcoholic. In addition to the medical causes of death that are directly related to chemical dependence, alcoholics are 10 times more likely than non-alcoholics to die from fires, 5 to 13 times more likely to die from falls, and 6 to 15 times more likely to commit suicide.

Over 50 percent of all highway fatalitites involve drunk driving — the leading single cause of death among 15 to 24 year olds. This is especially scary when we learn where kids go to turn on. (According to the PRIDE survey, "home," "a friend's house," and "other places" are the first three most popular places; "the car" is fourth.)

6. Chemical dependence is a treatable disease.

The five characteristics of chemical dependence just described — compulsive/obsessive, primary, progressive, chronic, and fatal — can be discouraging for both the addicted person and others who want to help. But there's a strong, bright light at the end of the tunnel: Chemical dependence can be treated and arrested.

Seven out of ten chemically dependent persons who accept treatment and use the knowledge and tools they are given there find sobriety. Perhaps one out of ten seeks treatment on his or her own, but usually not before losing almost everything of value. The others get there because the people around them care enough to intervene.

A big problem with chemical dependence is the fact that denial is one of its chief symptoms. The addict is the last person to know and accept that he or she is sick. Chemical dependence has been described as "the disease that tells people they don't have a disease." And that is why intervention must come from the outside, from significant persons surrounding the addict: family, friends, teachers, employers, and other concerned individuals.

Notes

1. George E. Vaillant, M.D., *The Natural History of Alcoholism: Causes, Patterns, and Paths to Recovery* (Cambridge, MA: Harvard University Press, 1983), p. 3.

2. *The Addiction Letter*, Vol. 3, No. 4 (April 1987).

CHAPTER

4

The Feeling Disease

Chemical dependence is also called "the feeling disease." Dr. Vernon E. Johnson, founder of the Johnson Institute, has done much to explain the disease on the emotional level. He describes it in terms of a four-phase progression.*

Phase I: Learns Mood Swing

A person is introduced to alcohol or another drug and discovers that it has the power to produce a mood swing. The mood swing is experienced as positive, fun, and rewarding. There is no pain, emotional cost, or unpleasant consequence associated with using.

The person begins to trust alcohol/drugs. He or she learns that they are reliable and quick. They work every time! He or she also learns that the degree of the mood swing can be controlled, depending on how much of the chemical is used. ("One drink makes me feel good; two or three make me feel even better!")

When the high wears off — and this is important — the person returns to normal feelings and normal living.

---

* These phases are only briefly summarized here. For more detailed descriptions, see Vernon Johnson's books, *Intervention: How To Help Someone Who Doesn't Want Help* (Minneapolis: Johnson Institute, 1986) and *I'll Quit Tomorrow: A Practical Guide to Alcoholism Treatment* (San Francisco: Harper & Row, 1980).

Phase II: Seeks Mood Swing

The person now applies what he or she has learned in Phase I to social situations — parties, entertaining friends, business luncheons, holiday celebrations. He or she has gone from *learning how to use alcohol/drugs* to *forming a relationship with alcohol/drugs.*

The person starts making some self-imposed rules to govern his or her use of chemicals. For example: "I'll *only* drink at parties (or at home)," "I'll *never* drink on weekdays or before 5 p.m.," "I'll *only* have two or three drinks at a time."

During this stage, the person starts paying a price for alcohol/drug use: hangovers, a fuzzy head, a feeling of not being on top of things. It passes. The person is willing to pay that price and repeats the behavior that leads to it. He or she starts to anticipate using (TGIF) and may develop a regular ritual of using ("just one drink before dinner").

Again, as in Phase I, the person can and does return to normal feelings and normal living after the high wears off.

Most so-called "social drinkers/drug users" remain in Phase II. So do many misusers and abusers. The point is, they can still choose and control their using.

Phase III: Harmful Dependence

This phase signals the presence of the disease of chemical dependence. Nobody knows why some people progress to it and others don't. We do know, however, what happens when they do.

The person begins to suffer losses in his or her life that are directly related to the alcohol/drug use. These losses occur at all levels: emotional, mental, spiritual, social, vocational, physical, even economic or financial. They can be seen in the behavior changes that take place and the delusional system that develops.

Behavior changes include a more intense preoccupation with alcohol/drugs, a growing rigidity around rituals of using, increased tolerance, more ingenuity in getting and using the chemicals, and repeated breaking of self-imposed rules.

The delusional system that develops is made up of a powerful set of psychological defenses (denial, rationalization, projection, and minimizing) plus memory distortions (repression, blackouts, and euphoric recall) that combine to prevent the chemical dependent from consciously experiencing the pain he or she is feeling.

The defense system is the result of the high emotional costs that using exacts during this phase: painful feelings of remorse, guilt, shame, anger, hurt, free-floating anxiety, self-hatred, and eventually despair and suicidal thoughts. Because nobody can willingly live with such pain day in and day out, the psychological defenses come to the rescue: denial ("I do NOT have a problem with drugs"), rationalization ("If I didn't have so many problems, I wouldn't use"), projection ("If you'd leave me alone, I'd stop using. . .it's YOUR fault!"), and minimizing ("I only had a couple of beers").

These defenses lock the pain inside; the continued use of chemicals keeps it locked inside and provides the only relief.

The person starts experiencing memory distortions through chemically-induced blackouts, psychologically-induced repression, and euphoric recall ("What do you mean, I was loaded last night? I was just fine!"). These memory distortions literally destroy the person's ability to remember what happened during any given drinking or using episode.

Finally, family members, friends, and employers become enablers who support the delusional system of the chemical dependent by reacting to the person's behavior in ways that keep him or her from experiencing his or her own pain.

The person is out of touch with reality on two fronts. The delusional system prevents him or her from recognizing or acknowledging what is happening, and so do the enablers around him or her.

This is the middle stage of addiction.

Phase IV: Drinks/Uses to Feel Normal

The person in Phase IV uses alcohol/drugs to feel normal — or what he or she remembers as normal. Deterioration continues in all areas of his or her life. Relief, when it is found, is temporary. The emotional pain is overwhelming. Thoughts of suicide occur, and attempts may be made.

This is the late stage of addiction. Unless an intervention is done, the person will die prematurely.

It's an awful scenario with a terrible inevitability to it. *And it's not just the addict who suffers.* The people around the chemically dependent person — family, friends, coworkers — are also vulnerable to the effects of the disease.

Being in a relationship with an addict can leave you feeling angry, ashamed, hurt, afraid, uncertain, and lonely. To shield yourself from these feelings, you may strive for perfection, try to control the person's use of alcohol/drugs, or cover up your feelings with apathy and pretend not to care.

You may get so caught up in worrying about the addict that you forget your own needs. Your self-esteem may plummet. You may become depressed or develop any number of stress-related illnesses. You may start abusing chemicals yourself as a means of escape.

You will almost certainly feel some sense of guilt, either because you feel powerless to help or because you believe that you are to blame. (Imagine the guilt parents and siblings feel when a teenage addict commits suicide!)

In other words, there are at least two people who stand to benefit greatly from your intervening with a teenager who is using alcohol/drugs: the teenager, and you.

CHAPTER

5

How Chemical Dependence in Teenagers Differs from Chemical Dependence in Adults

Most of what we know about chemical dependence was learned from studying and working with adults. Much of that information is relevant to teenage chemical dependence. But there are important differences between adult users and adolescent users, and we must understand those differences before we can help teenagers in trouble with alcohol/drugs.

1. Polydrug use is higher among teenagers than adults.

Adults tend to find and "stay faithful" to one or two mood-altering chemicals. Teenagers are likely to use anything that's available.

Alcohol is the #1 drug of choice and the most widely abused among both populations. In fact, alcohol is the "drug of entry" into the whole drug scene. For teens, marijuana is #2, and cocaine is quickly becoming #3 in many parts of the country. As recent surveys show, the other drugs — uppers, downers, hallucinogens — are still around.

Teenagers tend not to be very picky about what they will and won't use. Since everything but alcohol is illegal, one can never be too sure of what one is buying, and many kids don't bother to ask.

There is no "truth in packaging" on the streets. It isn't

unusual to find pot mixed with PCP (an animal tranquilizer), cocaine or heroin laced with strychnine (a rat poison), or grocery store mushrooms mixed with LSD (a hallucinogen).

Also, it is believed that the THC (the active ingredient) in marijuana today is ten times more powerful than in the 1970s, so it's easier to get hooked on less.

The characteristics of chemical dependence are similar for both adults and teenagers. And it doesn't make any difference which chemical one becomes dependent on; the addiction process is the same.

But young people are apt to use many more different types of chemicals than adults, and this makes it more difficult to tell what and how much they're on.

2. The reasons teenagers use alcohol/drugs are more "internal" than the reasons adults use.

Generally speaking, adults drink and use for more "external" reasons — the boss, the kids, the spouse, the occasion. Many women blame a stressful life event (such as a death or divorce) for their chemical abuse.

Young people, in contrast, use alcohol/drugs to have fun, to feel better or stronger, to have more confidence on dates, and other "internal" reasons. Also, young people will admit to the goal of getting high or drunk when they party ("Let's get wasted tonight!"). Most adults won't admit to anything of the sort, even if it's true. They call it "socializing."

3. The levels of use are harder to determine for teenagers than adults.

When dealing with teenagers, it is very difficult to distinguish between the abuse level and the early stages of addiction. What are considered symptoms of chemical dependence in adults are often nothing more than "adolescent behaviors" in some teens.

For example, one symptom of chronic late-stage chemical dependence in adults is using alcohol/drugs in the morning. They usually do this to stave off "withdrawal" — the shakes, nausea, and other unpleasant physical and emotional feelings. They may need alcohol/drugs to feel normal and be able to function at home or on the job.

In contrast, many teenagers at the abuse level can and often do use alcohol/drugs in the morning. Going to school high, stoned, or drunk is the thing to do. Thus what is always a sign of chemical dependence in adults is sometimes, but not always, a sign of chemical dependence in teenagers.

Here's another example: When adults hide their alcohol/drugs from family, friends, and coworkers, it's a definite symptom of chemical dependence. In contrast, almost all teenagers who use chemicals hide them at one time or another, usually because of the legal implications or to avoid parental hassles or getting caught by the authorities. Again, what is *always* a sign of chemical dependence in adults *isn't* always a reliable indicator among teenagers.

Other symptoms vary, too. Young people don't have jobs to lose or marriages to break up, and they seldom experience the chronic physical effects adult users do. Furthermore, what may *look* like symptoms in adolescents may be special education concerns (such as poor concentration skills, moodiness, hyperactivity, or poor social skills) or behaviors traceable to growing up in an alcoholic home.*

---

* To learn more about feelings and behaviors of teenagers from alcoholic homes, read *Different Like Me: A Book for Teens Who Worry About Their Parents' Use of Alcohol/Drugs* by Evelyn Leite and Pamela Espeland (Minneapolis: Johnson Institute, 1987).

4. The four phases of the feeling disease are not as applicable to youth as they are to adults.

What is considered "social use" among adults in Phase II (Seeks Mood Swing) is always "misuse" among teenagers because they are breaking the law.

For adults, Phase III (Harmful Dependence) signals the beginning of chemical dependence. Since it is so hard with adolescents to distinguish between chemical abuse and early stage chemical dependence symptoms, it is better to call this phase "Harmfully Involved" and to put chemical dependence in Phase IV (Drinks/Uses to Feel Normal). And since the average adolescent doesn't know what "normal" feelings are, it is better to call this fourth phase "Harmfully Dependent" when applying it to youth.

Here, then, are the differences in the feeling disease among adults and adolescents:

Adult Feeling Disease Phases	Adolescent Feeling Disease Phases
I. Learns Mood Swing	I. Learns Mood Swing
II. Seeks Mood Swing	II. Seeks Mood Swing
III. Harmful Dependence	III. Harmfully Involved
IV. Drinks/Uses to Feel Normal	IV. Harmfully Dependent

5. Although the addiction process is similar for adults and teenagers, it happens more quickly with teenagers.

Experience shows that it can take from eight to ten years for a 30-year-old white male to reach the chronic stages of alcoholism from the time he begins using alcohol to meet his needs. (It takes less time for females.) For a young person under age 15 who is abusing the same amount of alcohol, it can take fewer than 15 months.

Cocaine gives such an extreme euphoric high that people literally "fall in love" with it and move almost immediately from misuse to abuse. Crack — a form of cocaine which is smoked rather than snorted — works so quickly that a user gets high in seconds. When it comes to creating addicts, crack appears to be the most efficient drug of all.

Young people are especially attracted to crack because of its low cost and widespread availability. In some parts of the country, it is now the #2 drug of choice, second to alcohol.

6. The emotional arrestment of chemical dependence takes place earlier in teenagers than adults.

When one begins to abuse chemicals by getting drunk or high, his or her emotional development is arrested. He or she becomes incapable of working through grief or negative feelings or working on relationships.

Many teenagers who stop using are *pre-teens* emotionally. Unlike most adults, they have no emotional development to fall back on. All of the tasks of adolescence are still before them. Adults often remember "how good it was" before they became chemically dependent; teenagers don't have those memories.

Many teenage addicts never had the time to develop life skills. Rather than talk about adolescents in terms of "rehabilitation," we should use the term "habilitation," since what we end up doing is teaching them how to live.

7. While the delusional system is similar in adults and teenagers, it seems to be more complicated in teenagers.

Chemically dependent adults and teens alike are out of touch with reality due to the denial, rationalization, projection, minimizing, and memory distortions that characterize the delusional system. Young people have another strike against them: their age. It is very difficult for a teen to accept that he or she is chemically dependent when "everyone knows" that alcoholics are guys over 50 who live on Skid Row.

Another factor that strengthens the delusional system for many adolescents is the presence of THC in their bloodstreams. THC is sometimes used to prevent nausea in cancer patients undergoing chemotherapy. Many teens who smoke marijuana or hashish regularly and also drink alcohol rarely experience hangovers. And since "everyone knows" that alcoholics get hangovers, they themselves can't possibly be alcoholics — or so their reasoning goes.

The teenager who is naturally imaginative and creative (or wishes he or she were) has another deluding temptation to contend with. Cocaine, marijuana, and some of the hallucinogens can lead one to believe that he or she is *more* creative under the influence. The high is identified with being a better musician, artist, writer, even a better lover. It's not uncommon for teens to use drugs prior to tests, athletic events, performances, and other occasions when they must do their best. They think the drugs will help them.

8. Teenagers have more "built-in" enablers than adults.

First and foremost, young people have enablers called PARENTS. For many of us, taking responsibility for our children's behavior is as natural as breathing. When they succeed, we strut around feeling proud. And when they fail, we feel as if it's somehow our fault.

I know a farmer with a 23-year-old son who has cost him $35,000 in fines for driving while intoxicated, car accidents, and broken machinery. Every time the son gets arrested, the father is the first to bail him out and pay his bills. When I asked him how long he planned on doing that, all he said was,

"He is my son, you know."

For many youth workers — especially teachers, ministers, and counselors who invest a lot of their time and energy in children — the parent in them gets hooked, even if they don't have kids of their own. They, too, become enablers.

Plus the parents of the friends of the chemically dependent teen get involved. They may be either "for" or "against," but they climb into the ring along with everyone else.

In general, youth tend to have far more enablers than adults. The average chemically dependent adult might have as many as 10 to 12 enablers — family, friends, in-laws, the family doctor, the boss, and maybe the court. In contrast, the average chemically dependent teenager might have 50-60 enablers — immediate family, grandparents, uncles, aunts, school personnel, church staff, law-enforcement officers, court personnel, medical staff, friends, and parents of friends — all making it easier for the teenager to keep using!

Back to parents for a moment: It is *much* more difficult for parents to stop enabling their children than it is for spouses and friends to stop enabling other adults. I've met many ex-spouses and ex-friends, but I've never met an ex-parent (or an ex-kid). Our children are our children forever.

This is also true for many step-parents and foster parents. And that's why it's so hard not to be an enabler if your son or daughter is using alcohol/drugs.

6

From Use to Addiction: An Overview of Teenage Involvement with Alcohol/Drugs

We know that the addiction process has four levels, and that the feeling disease has four phases. Here is how they relate for teenagers:

The Addiction Process	*The Feeling Disease*	
Level 1: USE ⟷	Phase I:	Learns Mood Swing
Level 2: MISUSE ⟷	Phase II:	Seeks Mood Swing
Level 3: ABUSE ⟷	Phase III:	Harmfully Involved
Level 4: ADDICTION ⟷	Phase IV:	Harmfully Dependent

The kind of intervention you will do will depend on which level a teenager is at.

Each level of use is distinguished by certain *characteristics, chemicals of choice,* and *consequences of using.* This information can help you to assess a teenager's position and determine which intervention approach is most likely to succeed.

Level 1: Use ⟷ Phase I: Learns Mood Swing

The teenager has his or her first experiences with alcohol/ drugs and uses them occasionally. At this level, his or her tolerance to alcohol/drugs is low; it doesn't take much to feel the effects.

Characteristics of Level 1 Use

• **Acceptable**

Uses alcohol/drugs with parental knowledge.

1. in the family setting (at holiday meals and celebrations; in keeping with ethnic customs). Frequency: 4-6 times a year.
2. in the liturgical setting (taking communion at church; observing religious rites at church, temple, or home). Frequency: varies.
3. for medical reasons (with a doctor's prescription; with parental supervision or at the individual's discretion). Frequency: varies.

• **Experimental**

Uses alcohol/drugs *without* parental knowledge — sometimes alone, more often with friends. Frequency: varies.

Level 1 Chemicals of Choice

• **alcohol**

Mostly beer and wine, wine coolers, sometimes hard liquor.

• **marijuana**

Usually locally grown.

• **over-the-counter medications, pills or liquids**

Asthma, hay fever, or cold remedies that contain alcohol or antihistamines. Other drugs that stimulate, cause drowsiness, or dizziness: NoDoz, Nyquil, Actifed, Sudafed, Dramamine, Sominex.

• **inhalants**

Glue, solvents, aerosols, Liquid Paper, Rush (PARENTS: for your information, Rush is an over-the-counter stimulant sold in "head shops" that comes in a vial-like bottle and is sniffed).

Level 1 Consequences of Using

• **Social**
Few if any. First episode of intoxication or first drug-related high.

• **Personal**
Few if any, with the exception of toxic inhalants.* First hangover.

Level 2: Misuse ⟵⟶ Phase II: Seeks Mood Swing

The teenager uses alcohol/drugs regularly, but usually only on the weekends (or even less often). His or her tolerance increases.

Characteristics of Level 2 Use

• Control and choice are still present. Can decide when and whether to use and how much to use.
• Begins to develop pattern of use, but weeknight use is still the exception.
• Starts devising reasons for using without parental permission and at other than acceptable occasions (described above for Level 1). Examples: to impress friends, to "get ready" for a social occasion, to "relax" after a hard day.
• Starts making self-imposed rules to govern using. Examples: "I'll only drink at parties," "I'll only have two drinks," "I'll smoke pot, but I won't smoke hash," "I'll only get drunk on weekends."

---

* *Immediate* effects for some who use toxic inhalants may include heart failure, death by suffocation or depression of the central nervous system, nausea, sneezing, coughing, nosebleeds, loss of appetite, lack of coordination.

Level 2 Chemicals of Choice

- **alcohol**

Uses hard liquor — whiskey, gin, vodka, rum — more frequently.

- **marijuana**

Prefers foreign-grown. May also use hashish, hash oil.

- **uppers/downers**

Amphetamines, tranquilizers, and sedatives: Dexadrine, Benzedrine, Valium, Librium, Quaaludes, Dalmane.

- **hallucinogens**

Natural ones such as psilocybin (mushrooms) and peyote.

- **cocaine**

Experiments with by snorting; may try smoking crack for the first time.

Level 2 Consequences of Using

- **Social**

Legal: Is now breaking the law and runs the risk of getting caught. May experience first arrest for MIP (Minor In Possession).

School: Activities begin to suffer, suspension from extracurricular activities may result, truancy begins. Problems with tardiness, handing in homework late (or not at all). Avoids teachers and leaves the classroom more often.

Home: Starts sneaking out at night and gives vague explanations or lies about whereabouts and activities. Becomes less responsible about chores.

Friends: Feels strong peer pressure to use at social events. Associates mainly with other users.

- **Personal**

Physical: Hangovers continue; "bad trips" (very unpleasant experiences with alcohol/drugs) may begin. Trouble sleeping on weekends.

Mental: Spends more time and energy planning the next high; equates social occasions with getting high. Starts minimizing extent of usage. Denies (lies to parents) and makes excuses for using and behavior.

Emotional: Severe and unexplainable mood swings. Normal emotional tasks (grieving, dealing with relationship issues) are delayed.

Spiritual: Family values and drug values come into conflict. Questions the need to go to church or temple.

Level 3: Abuse ◄──────► Phase III: Harmfully Involved (or Early Stage of Addiction)

The teenager is preoccupied with alcohol/drugs and uses 2-3 times a week and on weekends. His or her tolerance continues to increase.

Characteristics of Level 3 Use

- Has less control and choice over whether to use.
- Rituals for using are established. Examples: getting high after school, smoking marijuana while listening to music, weekend keg parties. Begins to acquire and use drug paraphernalia (pipes, bongs, one-hitters, roach clips).
- Starts anticipating and planning times and occasions when he or she can use alcohol/drugs.
- Becomes more ingenious about hiding use from parents and deceiving authorities. Examples: staying overnight with friends, coming home and going straight to his or her room, avoiding family meals, having parties at home when parents are on vacation, not showing up at family activities.
- Solitary use begins. Examples: Drinks alone in room at

home; smokes marijuana in room with window open; uses on the way to or from school or work.

- Self-imposed rules are modified and more exceptions are allowed. ("I'll only drink on Mondays and Wednesdays and at weekend parties," "I won't drink on the job but only after work," "I won't get high at school — but I'll skip school to get high if my friends do.")
- Makes repeated promises to family and authorities about cutting down or quitting.

Level 3 Chemicals of Choice

- **alcohol**
Prefers hard liquor.
- **marijuana**
Prefers seedless, if available.
- **uppers/downers**
"Speed" (White Crosses) and barbiturates (Seconal, Nembutal, Tuinal).
- **hallucinogens**
Synthetics including PCP ("angel dust"), LSD ("acid"), MDA (methyl dioxyamphetamine), mescaline.
- **cocaine**
Snorts more regularly; uses crack more than once.
- **"designer drugs"**
Examples include MDMA (a compounded form of methamphetamine called "Ecstasy"), MDEA (a slightly altered form of Ecstasy called "Eve").

Level 3 Consequences of Using

- **Social**
Legal: Shoplifting, vandalism, dealing drugs, accumulating drug paraphernalia. May run away from home. First arrest for driving while intoxicated (DWI).

School: Grades drop and truancy becomes more frequent. Starts sleeping in class, has a marked change in attitude, and may be suspended from school. Brings drugs to school; forges passes and excuses for absences.

Home: Experiences money problems; may steal from parents. Spends more time in his or her room with the door closed; stays out overnight. Becomes verbally and sometimes physically abusive. There are more family fights. Promises to change.

Friends: All are using friends. Drops any remaining straight friends.

- **Personal**

Physical: Injuries, respiratory problems, weight loss or gain, overdoses. Personal hygiene suffers; doesn't bathe as often and isn't as concerned about the appearance of his or her clothes, hair, and skin.

Mental: Blackouts begin. (Not to be confused with passing out, a blackout is a period of seconds, minutes, hours, or even days during which the user is awake and active but later remembers nothing about the events that took place.) Has a shorter attention span and decreased motivation/drive. Starts rationalizing alcohol/drug use and blaming others.

Emotional: Depression; suicidal thoughts. Feels different from his or her friends and cut off from them. Anger, loneliness, hurt, feelings of inferiority, a sense of worthlessness.

Spiritual: The conflict between family values and drug values grows more severe and causes shame and guilt. May stop going to church or temple.

Level 4: Addiction $\longleftrightarrow$ Phase IV: Harmfully Dependent (Middle and Late Stages of Addiction)

The teenager uses alcohol/drugs compulsively, usually daily. His or her tolerance continues to increase.

Characteristics of Level 4 Use

- Can no longer exercise control or choice over his or her alcohol/drug use. Can no longer predict how much he or she will use or what the outcome will be.
- More rituals; rituals become more rigid. Examples: uses in the morning before school or work, during the lunch hour and school breaks .
- Binge use — may remain intoxicated or high throughout the day for two or more days.
- Exhibits grandiose and aggressive behavior. More defiant in school. More risk-taking with police. Physically violent with family members and friends.
- Obsessed with alcohol/drugs and the need to keep a constant supply on hand. Never uses all of supply with friends. Stocks up on liquor for Sundays; spends a lot of time getting drugs; when dealing, "shorts" customers and keeps part for self.
- Becomes more careless about hiding drugs and paraphernalia. Isn't aware of self as high, so memory and judgment are impaired. Uses more recklessly; leaves pipes and drugs in bedroom without hiding them.
- Solitary use increases in amount and frequency.
- Abandons self-imposed rules. Because of the obsession and the compulsion to use, life becomes alcohol/drug-centered. The "love affair" is all-encompassing. Everything else becomes secondary to using.
- Makes repeated efforts to control or reduce excessive use.

Level 4 Chemicals of Choice

- **alcohol** (still #1!)
- **any other available drug:**
uppers/downers, hallucinogens, cocaine.
- **narcotics** (for some)
Codeine, Percodan, morphine, heroin.
- **crack**
Smokes regularly.

The needle may be used for some of the drugs.

Level 4 Consequences of Using

- **Social**

Legal: Commits crimes such as breaking and entering, robbery, assault and battery, and prostitution. May deal drugs more frequently and in larger quantities, engages in physical violence, and spends more time in jail.

School: May sell drugs at school. Use during school hours is common. May be suspended or expelled; may vandalize the school. May be fired or change jobs.

Home: Family fights become more physical. Stays away from home for longer periods of time or may leave altogether. Parents may threaten to kick him or her out.

Friends: Using friends may show their concern. Responds by avoiding them and may use violence against them. Tries a "geographic escape" by going to places where friends are not likely to be.

- **Personal**

Physical: More injuries; chronic cough; more severe weight loss; tremors (shaky hands, jerky movements); dry heaves. Withdrawal symptoms. Rapid deterioration of health and appearance.

Mental: Projects self-hatred onto others. Impaired memory; flashbacks (feelings of being under the influence of alcohol/drugs even when none have been recently ingested). Regular blackouts.

Emotional: Deep remorse and despair; suicide plans and attempts; feelings of paranoia (of being watched or "chased" or under suspicion); undefinable fears.

Spiritual: Complete "spiritual bankruptcy" — the conflict between values and behaviors becomes subconscious and no longer serves to restrain or inhibit using behavior. No peace even when high. Constant, overwhelming feelings of self-hatred, hopelessness and helplessness.

7

How to Tell If A Teenager is Using — And How Bad It Really Is

Now that you know something about teenage alcohol/drug use, you can put your knowledge to work. You can use what you have learned to determine whether a teenager you know is using alcohol/drugs, and, if so, the probable level of usage he or she is currently at.

The following questionnaire is not a diagnostic tool. Rather, it is an *assessment* tool that will give you an idea of where things stand.

For the sake of simplicity, the questionnaire has been written to parents. Teachers and other professionals, please make whatever modifications are necessary.

Some questions have more than one part. Answer each question with a "yes" or "no." (IMPORTANT: Even if you can answer "yes" to only one part of a question with many parts, answer the whole question with a "yes.")

Section I

YES NO

___ ___ 1. Has your child ever been arrested on a MIP (Minor In Possession) charge or been at a party broken up by the police?

___ ___ 2. Has your child ever been suspended from school activities for using alcohol/drugs or skipping classes? Does he or she have a poor attitude about school and/or family life? Has he or she dropped activities that used to be important to him or her?

___ ___ 3. Is your child becoming less responsible around the house with regard to regular chores or curfews? Have you ever caught your child sneaking out of the house at night?

___ ___ 4. Do your child's friends drink or smoke marijuana?

___ ___ 5. Has your child ever experienced a hangover or a bad trip due to alcohol/drug use? Have you smelled alcohol or pot on your child's breath or in his or her room?

___ ___ 6. Has your child lied to you about his or her activities and friends, or made excuses about drinking/using behaviors (his or her own or friends')?

___ ___ 7. Has your child exhibited any unexplainable mood changes or emotional ups and down that seem excessive to you?

___ ___ 8. Does your child question your values about drinking/drug use? Does he or she challenge or question the importance of family activities and church/temple attendance?

___ ___ 9. Does your child volunteer to clean up after adult parties where alcohol was served, even if he or she isn't being responsible about other chores around the house?

___ ___ 10. Have you ever been embarrassed enough by these behaviors that you've made excuses about your child to the court, the school, friends, or even members of your family?

Section II

YES NO

___ ___ 11. Has your child ever been arrested for shoplifting, vandalism, driving while intoxicated (DWI), or possession of alcohol/drugs? Have you found empty beer, wine, or liquor bottles, drugs, or drug paraphernalia (papers, pipes, or clips — used for holding marijuana cigarettes) in your child's room?

___ ___ 12. Has your child ever been suspended from school for possession of alcohol/drugs or fighting? Have any of the following occurred frequently: sleeping in school, falling grades, truancy, forging passes, forging excuses from you about missed classes or days?

___ ___ 13. Are you missing any money or objects from the house that could be sold for money? Is your liquor supply down? Has there been more than the usual amount of verbal fighting and arguing? Is your child being more secretive or spending more time in his or her room with the door closed or locked? Has he or she been staying out all night?

___ ___ 14. Has your child changed friends from those who don't use alcohol/drugs to those who do?

___ ___ 15. Has your child experienced a significant weight loss or gain, unexplained injuries, respiratory problems, or overdoses? Has his or her appearance become sloppy; does he or she seem less concerned with personal hygiene?

___ ___ 16. Has your child's attention span noticeably decreased? Does he or she have less motivation or drive than in previous times? Does he or she blame others more frequently? Has he or she had memory lapses — times when he or she couldn't remember going somewhere or doing something?

___ ___ 17. Has your child been depressed or voiced feelings of hopelessness and worthlessness? Has he or she been saying things like "I wish I were dead" or "Life isn't worth living"?

___ ___ 18. Has your child argued with you about basic family, educational, or religious values? Has he or she stopped going to church or participating in family activities?

___ ___ 19. Does your child strongly defend his or her right to drink or use drugs?

___ ___ 20. Have you ever felt used or taken advantage of by your child — especially at times when you ended up blaming the school, the court, or his or her friends for his or her problems?

Section III

YES NO

___ ___ 21. Has your child ever been arrested for robbery, drug dealing, assault and battery, vandalism, or prostitution?

___ ___ 22. Has your child been suspended from school more than once or expelled? Has he or she been fired from a job?

___ ___ 23. Has your child ever gotten physically violent with you? Has he or she stayed away from home for more than a weekend, or even left home "for good"?

___ ___ 24. Has your child gotten violent with his or her

friends, or started avoiding them to the point where they have begun expressing some concern?

___ ___ 25. Have you noticed more weight loss or injuries in your child? What about overdoses, tremors, dry heaves, or chronic coughing?

___ ___ 26. Does your child blame you, his or her friends, and just about anybody else for his or her problems? Does he or she show a lot of anger? Are you aware of more times when your child can't seem to remember things that he or she has said or done?

___ ___ 27. Has your child ever made suicide plans, left notes, or actually attempted suicide? Have you noticed him or her exhibiting feelings of paranoia?

___ ___ 28. Would you describe your child as being "spiritually bankrupt"?

___ ___ 29. Does your child "turn off" to talks about alcohol/drug abuse or skip classes about them, dismissing them as "a bore" or "a drag"? When confronted with evidence that you know about his or her alcohol/drug use, does he or she still deny having problems with using?

___ ___ 30. Are you afraid for your child's safety — or even your child's life — because of any of the behaviors and consequences described in this questionnaire?

What Your Responses Mean

- "Yes" answers to questions 1-10 indicate that your child is probably at Level 2 of the addiction process. He or she is *misusing* alcohol/drugs and seeking the mood swing.

- "Yes" answers to questions 11-20 indicate that your child is probably at Level 3 of the addiction process. He or she is *abusing* alcohol/drugs and is harmfully involved with them. He or she might also be in the early stages of addiction.
- "Yes" answers to questions 21-30 indicate that your child is probably at Level 4 of the addiction process. He or she is *addicted to* alcohol/drugs and is harmfully dependent on them.

None of this is good news. It hurts to learn that your child is in trouble with alcohol/drugs. It hurts to see what alcohol/drug use can do to a teenager. It hurts to feel powerless to stop it, as many parents do.

But you are *not* powerless. You *can* put a stop to the progress of the disease of chemical dependence in your son or daughter. Working together with other caring persons, you can arrest the disease and head your child toward recovery.

A WORKING DEFINITION OF CHEMICAL DEPENDENCE

If the use of alcohol/drugs is interfering with any area of a person's life — whether *social* (legal, school/work, family, or friends) or *personal* (physical, mental, emotional, or spiritual) — and he or she *cannot stop using without help,* then he or she is chemically dependent.

CHAPTER

8

The Tasks of Adolescence

It's a terrible thing to discover that a teenager is dependent on alcohol/drugs. And given the harmful effects that addiction has on one's life, it's natural to wonder, "Why doesn't he or she just QUIT?"

The answer is simple: Because he or she can't.

Chemically dependent people don't know that they have a problem. They can't see what's happening to them. They are *out of touch with reality* — delusional. Chemically dependent people are the last to realize that they have a disease, much less admit it — and much less do something about it.

That is why intervention is necessary. During intervention, people who *can* see what's happening present reality to the person who can't in a *receivable* way. As Vernon Johnson explains in his book, *Intervention,* "By 'presenting reality,' we mean presenting *specific facts* about the person's behavior and the things that have happened because of it. 'A receivable way' is one that the person cannot resist because it is *objective, unequivocal, nonjudgmental,* and *caring*"[1].

Generally speaking, teenagers tend to be more out of touch with reality than adults simply because they're teenagers. Adolescence is a time of confusion and uncertainty. The fundamental reality of "Who am I?" has not yet been established. Finding an answer is what adolescence is all about. In fact, adolescence has been called the "stage of identity."[2]

To intervene effectively with teenagers who are using alcohol/drugs, we must first have some understanding of adolescence — the transition between childhood and adulthood.

Some primitive cultures have formal rites of passage that mark this transition. Prior to the turn of the century, so did ours. Children worked side-by-side with their parents and other adults who served as role models, learning life skills and job skills from them. The passage to adulthood was a well-defined process that didn't take very long; being a teenager meant little more than being an adult in one's teens.

This is not true today. Adolescence has become a waiting period when one is neither a child nor an adult. Or, as many teenagers have complained, "I'm supposed to act like an adult, but you're treating me like a child!" To further complicate matters, the rites of passage are no longer clear.

For many teenagers, adulthood means a time when they can drive a car, drink alcohol or use other drugs, get a job, leave home, or become sexually active. Parents seem to offer little guidance in these areas, so teenagers turn to friends and peers who are just as confused as they are.

The rites of passage may not be clear, but the entry into adolescence couldn't be clearer. The sexual changes that take place are as subtle as being hit on the head with a hammer.

Think back on how you felt when these changes started happening to you. It's easy to forget how common it is for teenagers to feel confused, embarrassed, guilty, awkward, inferior, ugly, and scared.

At the same time, adolescents have feelings of invulnerability and immortality that lead them to behave in reckless ways. An "it-can't-happen-to-me" attitude prevails as they drive too fast ("I'll never have an accident"), have their first sexual experiences ("I'll never get pregnant or get AIDS"), and experiment with drugs ("I'll never get hooked").

This physical and emotional jumble is joined by the inability to look ahead and visualize the long-term effects of present behaviors. To tell a teenager who is skipping classes that he or she might not be admitted to college someday is virtually meaningless. For many, *today* is what matters.

Considering all that adolescents have to deal with, it's no wonder that being out of touch with reality goes with the job!

In many respects, adolescence *is* a job — something to be accomplished, not merely endured. Child development professionals have identified four distinct tasks of adolescence — tasks that must be accomplished in order for the teenager to establish his or her identity. Coupled with these are four basic needs. Understanding these tasks and self-esteem needs can bring us closer to understanding adolescence.

Task 1: To Determine One's Vocation

Accomplishing this task gives *meaning* to one's life.

It includes choosing one's life work and getting the necessary training — going to trade school or college, joining the military, and so on.

Underlying this task is the self-esteem need *to be somebody*. This need is best met by doing things and experiencing some success.

The goal of this task is *to achieve independence*. This means that one must acquire competence in life skills and job skills with the aim of someday being self-supporting.

Conflict with parents is normal with this task. Power struggles over curfew hours, activities, and chores are common. Some teenagers choose to work after school rather than take part in extracurricular activities. Some study less, and their grades drop. Some even quit school to work full-time.

When the self-esteem need to be somebody is met, one experiences positive feelings of strength, power, and competence.

Task 2: To Establish One's Values

Accomplishing this task gives *direction* to one's life. There is only one value that is intrinsic to all human beings: survival. The drive for self-preservation is built into each of us from birth. As we grow up, we learn other values from significant people close to us: to share, to work hard, to love others as we love ourselves, to serve our country, to worship God, and to respect nature. These are all imposed from the outside and must be internalized before we can start living them. Along the way, we question and challenge them.

Underlying this task is the self-esteem need *to go beyond* — to experience the spiritual. This need is best met by clarifying one's values.

The goal of this task is *to develop integrity*. This means that one must sort out one's values and choose which to keep and which to reject, what to believe in and how to believe.

Conflict with parents is normal with this task. Some teenagers question the need to formally worship God. Some question whether serving one's country must involve fighting for it. Some question the validity of the work ethic.

When the self-esteem need to go beyond is met, one experiences positive feelings of serenity, purpose, and peace of mind.

Task 3: To Explore One's Sexuality

Accomplishing this task gives *a sense of community* to one's life.

It includes examining one's roots (heritage) and one's relationship with both sexes (sexual orientation).

Underlying this task is the self-esteem need *to belong*. This need is best met by accepting one's maleness and femaleness.

The goal of this task is *to experience intimacy*. This means that one must develop the capacity to love and win the acceptance of one's peers.

Conflict with parents is normal with this task. Some teenagers want to date early or go steady. Some have a different sexual orientation than their parents want them to have. Some get involved in sexual relationships. And some prefer to spend time with friends their parents don't approve of.

When the self-esteem need to belong is met, one experiences positive feelings of warmth, trust, and at-one-ness.

Task 4: To Establish One's Authority

Accomplishing this task gives *uniqueness* to one's life.

It involves moving from being externally supported (by parents and other adults) to being internally supported (by oneself).

Underlying this task is the self-esteem need *to be oneself*. This need is best met by simply being.

The goal of this task is *to develop one's individuality*. This means that one must look at one's humanness, believe that he or she is special, and have an internal support system.

Conflict with parents is normal with this task. Some teenagers experiment with strange or unusual dress, or hairstyles. Some have different interests or hobbies than their parents wish they had. Some choose not to take part in family activities. And others just want to be alone, by themselves, without having to explain why.

When the self-esteem need to be oneself is met, one experiences positive feelings of being worthwhile, free, and secure.

If every adolescent managed to accomplish all four tasks and meet all four basic self-esteem needs, there would be far fewer troubled kids in the world. But the chances of this happening are remote. The self-esteem needs often aren't met, resulting in negative feelings and *emotional pain*.

- When the need to belong is not met, one can experience the negative feelings of being rejected, isolated, alienated, ugly, lonely, hurt, and unlovable.

- When the need to be somebody is not met, one can experience the negative feelings of being inferior, incompetent, a failure, confused, anxious, frustrated, stupid, and disgusted with oneself.
- When the need to be oneself is not met, one can experience the negative feelings of being insecure, fragile, embarrassed, vulnerable, awkward, scared, worthless, inadequate, and ashamed.
- When the need to go beyond is not met, one can experience the negative feelings of being depressed, hopeless, helpless, remorseful, despairing, guilty, and lost.

It is important to recognize that *low self-esteem is not unusual for the normal teenager*. Feelings change frequently during adolescence. Every teenager is capable of experiencing the negative feelings named above.

Adolescence is a time for one to work through these feelings, to discover that one doesn't have to be devastated by them, and to realize that one isn't unique in experiencing them. You've heard the saying, "No pain, no gain." It's true as far as it goes, but it skips an important step. The way it ought to go is, "No pain, *no struggle*, no gain." For while everyone experiences pain, not everyone grows. Growing requires us to struggle through the pain, not just bear with it — and especially not run from it.

Teenagers need to learn that negative feelings aren't bad. They're just negative. They make one feel uncomfortable. And this discomfort carries a message worth heeding: that one's basic self-esteem needs are not being met, and one had better do something to remedy that situation.

As parents, teachers, helping professionals, and youth workers, we must encourage teenagers to express their feelings appropriately — to state openly what they need, want, and expect. We must help them to understand that feelings change. We must let them know that expressing one's feelings brings relief; that negative feelings let out into the open air begin to dissipate, and one can then start identifying and working on the unmet needs that caused them. We must teach teenagers that negative feelings can change to positive when the self-esteem needs are satisfied.

The growing pains of adolescence make it hard to meet those needs. It's hard to get down to the business of establishing one's identity when one's body is under siege from within, one's emotions are riding a roller-coaster, and one simultaneously feels capable of doing anything and nothing. It's hard to think clearly and act rationally when one is suffering from emotional pain. And it's especially hard when one is out of touch with reality — often a common state of affairs for the average teenager.

But the average teenager eventually struggles through the pain, accomplishing the tasks and meeting the self-esteem needs and forming ties with reality. By the time he or she reaches adulthood, the question "Who am I?" is well on its way to being answered.

This is not the case for chemically dependent teenagers. Their emotional development is arrested. They are incapable of working through negative feelings. *All of the tasks of adolescence are still before them.* And they *stay out of touch with reality.*

A delusional system develops to keep the chemically dependent teenager out of touch with reality. And instead of the teenager growing, the system itself grows and deepens, layer by layer, until the teenager can no longer climb out of it by himself or herself. Intervention is the hand we can offer to lift the teenager up and out.

Notes

1. Vernon Johnson, *Intervention* (Minneapolis: The Johnson Institute, 1986), p. 61.
2. Erik H. Erikson, *Identity: Youth and Crisis* (New York: W.W. Norton & Company, Inc., 1968).

9

The Adolescent Delusional System

To deal with emotional pain, we all develop defenses. It's natural to want to protect ourselves from threatening or uncomfortable thoughts and feelings. This is a normal process that helps us to cope with fear, frustration, anxiety, and conflict.

We use defenses to "change" reality to avoid painful thoughts, painful feelings, threatening situations, and the unpleasant consequences of our own unacceptable behaviors.

Teenagers have four major defense strategies:

1. denial (refusing to recognize or accept reality),
2. projection (trying to make other people, places, or things responsible for one's unacceptable behavior; unloading one's self-hatred onto others)
3. rationalization (inventing excuses to make one's unacceptable behavior seem acceptable), and
4. minimizing (trying to make something look less serious than it is).

Another way to view adolescent defenses is in terms of "power plays" — games teenagers play when attempting to gain control of a situation and keep emotional pain at bay. These power plays come in four basic types: *avoider, blamer, controller,* and *protector.*

- **Avoider power plays** reflect the emotional pain of failing to meet the self-esteem need to belong. Teenagers who cannot meet this need feel rejected, alone, and hurt because they are not accepted and appreciated by others. So they refuse to accept the reality of their abilities, appearance, sexuality, family, or friends. This is what *denial* is all about: refusing to accept reality.

Avoider power plays include looking for attention, whining, and throwing up smokescreens to distract others (parents, teachers, helping professionals) from the real problem.

> *"I hate being a girl"* (*or boy*)
> *"I wish I lived with Susie's parents"*
> *"I don't have a problem"*
> *"Everybody else gets to stay out until 1 a.m."*
> *"I don't know how to do it — You do it for me"*
> *"I always have to do it. Why can't she"* (*or he*)
> *"It's no big deal!"*

• **Blamer power plays** reflect the emotional pain of failing to meet the self-esteem need to be somebody. Teenagers who cannot meet this need feel inferior and disgusted with themselves. So they try to pass their self-hatred on to others close to them. This is what *projection* is all about: unloading one's self-hatred onto others.

Blamer power plays include dumping, accusing, judging, threatening, and bullying.

> *"I hate you! I wish you weren't my parents!"*
> *"You are the meanest parents alive!"*
> *"You aren't like the other parents, who really care"*
> *"You better let me, or else!"*
> *"You will only make me do it more"*
> *"This place sucks!"*
> *"The teachers are out to get me"*
> *"The police are pigs"*

• **Controller power plays** reflect the emotional pain of failing to meet the self-esteem need to be oneself. Teenagers who cannot meet this need feel insecure, fragile, and ashamed. They question their own personal worth, even their own existence. So they make up "reasons" for their behavior and perceive any criticism as an attack. This is what *rationalization* is all about: inventing excuses for one's behavior.

Controller power plays include calculating, figuring you out, conning, and getting one up on you.

> *"Straight kids are a drag to be around"*
> *"Using friends are more fun and exciting"*
> *"My room is off limits. . .period!"*
> *"I don't have to tell you where I'm going"*
> *"School is boring. I can't stand the teachers"*
> *"I don't need to graduate anyway"*
> *"All the kids do it!"*
> *"It's my life! I'll live it the way I want!"*

• **Protector power plays** reflect the emotional pain of failing to meet the self-esteem need to go beyond. Teenagers who cannot meet this need feel helpless, hopeless, and guilty for not being "good enough." They look for others to make them feel good about themselves. So they tend to comply and do things so others will like them. This is what *minimizing* is all about: trying to make one's pain look less serious than it is.

Protector power plays include pleasing people, being nice, saying yes, and downplaying the seriousness of unacceptable behaviors.

> *"I only had a couple of wine coolers in the car"*
> *"It was only a little party"*
> *"Everything is just fine! Really!"*
> *"My boyfriend isn't that bad, Mom. He's had a hard time*

with his parents. You just have to understand him"
"Okay, Sis, I'll cover for you"
"I'll help you on the test this time, but next time you'd better study"
"Here's 10 bucks — it's all I have"

When normal teenagers engage in these power plays, their parents can usually confront them one-to-one and cut through the games. Even when they are using their defenses to mask their emotional pain, normal teenagers can still accept reality presented by concerned others and adjust their thinking accordingly. The defenses are up, but they're breachable.

This is also true for Level 1 users of alcohol/drugs who are learning the mood swing, and Level 2 misusers who are seeking the mood swing.

For example: Diane goes to a party where people are using alcohol and marijuana. Her parents have told her that such parties are off limits. She has rationalized her going by telling herself that all of her friends will be there and her parents will never find out. But the police come to break up the party, and Diane gets caught with a can of beer and charged with her first Minor in Possession (MIP) offense.

When confronted by her parents, she admits what she did and is willing to accept the consequences. She feels badly about violating her parents' trust, takes responsibility for breaking the law, and agrees to attend drug information classes at her school.

In contrast, Level 3 abusers who are harmfully involved, and Level 4 addicts who are harmfully dependent, are less able to accept reality presented by concerned others. Their defenses are far less breachable. They are out of touch with the reality of their behaviors and, in fact, their defenses serve to lock reality out while locking painful feelings in.

For example: Tom is arrested for driving while intoxicated

(DWI). When the police search his car, they find alcohol and cocaine. Later, faced with his parents, Tom denies that the drugs were his, blames the police for being "out to get him," rationalizes that "all the kids are doing it," and minimizes the extent of his usage ("I only had a couple of beers"). He agrees to attend DWI classes, but only to get the court off his back. He complies only to avoid spending time in jail.

Rigid defenses comprise the first layer of the delusional system of chemical dependence in adolescents.

The adolescent defenses of denial, projection, rationalization, and minimizing are the primary defenses for *all* chemically dependent persons. In time, they make it impossible for the alcoholic/addict to accept that he or she has a problem.

As the individual progresses through the levels of usage, these defenses are strengthened by three types of memory distortions: *blackouts, repression,* and *euphoric recall.* These combine to destroy the person's ability to remember what has happened during any drinking or using episode.

When normal teenagers with emotional pain use alcohol/ drugs, they discover that these chemicals can change their feelings. Relief from emotional pain is spelled "H-I-G-H." And getting high not only changes feelings — it also meets the four self-esteem needs.

- Chemicals allow you to be *somebody* no matter how inferior you feel or how much of a failure you think you are.
- Chemicals enable you *to go beyond* and escape the here-and-now no matter how hopeless or guilty you feel.
- Chemicals permit you *to belong* no matter how alone or rejected you feel.
- Chemicals invite you *to be yourself* no matter how insecure and worthless you feel.

Being able to meet these needs *without much effort* teaches one that chemicals are fun! During the early stages, using chemicals almost always results in temporary feelings of high self-esteem.

For the Level 2 teenager who seeks the mood swing, these feelings can be very seductive. It's great to be able to get a "quick fix" for emotional pain. The Level 3 teenager who is harmfully involved *counts on* chemicals to deliver these feelings. And the Level 4 teenager who is harmfully dependent *needs* chemicals to maintain these feelings.

Blackouts, repression, and euphoric recall usually begin at Level 3, although they can begin at earlier levels of use.

• A **blackout** is a chemically induced period of amnesia.

A blackout is often confused with passing out, but the two aren't the same — even though an alcohol/drug user can pass out *during* a blackout. Passing out means unconsciousness; the user appears to fall asleep abruptly. A blackout is different and usually has nothing to do with falling asleep.

People who experience blackouts cannot remember what they said or did during that period of seconds, minutes, hours, or days. From the outside, they may appear to be acting normally, but they will probably never be able to recall anything about the blackout — even under hypnosis.

One girl reported having blackouts for five seconds at a time, thinking that she was only "getting high."

One teenage boy left home in his car and woke up sleeping in a hotel lobby in another town. He bought a newspaper to find out where he was and what day it was. He discovered that he had lost ten days.

Blackouts usually occur in persons who have developed a high tolerance for alcohol/drugs. They almost never occur in non-dependent persons who use only moderate amounts.

• **Repression** is a psychologically induced period of amnesia.

Teenagers repress memories of unacceptable or shameful behaviors. We all do. It's normal, natural, and even healthy. None of us could bear the memory of *every* shameful or embarrassing moment we've experienced over a lifetime, so we repress, usually without suffering any harmful consequences. And we usually don't repeat the behavior or act that led to a particular painful memory.

Chemically dependent persons, in contrast, repeat shame-producing behaviors again and again. These may include driving while intoxicated, getting into accidents, abusing family members or friends, performing poorly at school or work, making passes at friends, vomiting in public, urinating in bed, and so on.

The more shameful acts one commits, the more memories one must repress, and, paradoxically, the more self-destructive one becomes — even to the point of committing suicide. Alcohol/drug abuse has been named a chief cause of the high suicide rate among teenagers today.

• **Euphoric recall** is a mystery.

Euphoric recall is the most difficult of the three memory distortions to understand. While blackouts and repression are both amnesia states — one doesn't remember what he or she did — euphoric recall allows for some *selective* memory of the unacceptable or shameful incident.

Chemically dependent persons will remember how they *felt*, but not how they *behaved*. And they will implicitly trust those memories as being accurate.

You can see this in an obviously intoxicated individual who thinks he can drive a car. Even though he is falling-down drunk, he will remember the next morning that he felt perfectly capable of driving. He is completely out of touch with the reality of his behavior.

Blackouts, repression, and euphoric recall comprise the second layer of the delusional system of chemical dependence in adolescents.

We know now that chemically dependent persons are cut off from reality — by their own subconscious defenses, and by the unconscious memory distortions of blackouts, repression, and euphoric recall.

We also know that chemically dependent persons usually are not cut off from the rest of humanity. They live among other people, many of whom function as enablers.

Enablers are people who react to chemically dependent persons in ways that effectively shield them from experiencing the harmful consequences of their alcohol/drug abuse. They take responsibility for and try to control the chemically dependent person's behaviors, feelings, and decisions. They sit on their blisters.

All chemically dependent persons have enablers. In fact, it is almost impossible to abuse alcohol/drugs without the help of enablers. Once chemicals take over, *somebody* has to take charge of the user's life!

Teenagers are even more protected by enablers than adults. And they don't need to be chemically dependent for others to step in and try to run their lives. They have the best, most committed, and most tireless enablers of all: their parents.

Enablers can be grouped into three basic types: *Provokers, Rescuers,* and *Victims.*

• Provokers react out of anger.

We get angry at our children because we care. We don't want to see them get hurt. So we try to control them, as if they were our possessions. We find it hard to let go and allow them to make mistakes. We are especially afraid for them when it comes to alcohol/drugs, for mistakes here could mean death.

Provoker behaviors include shouting and hollering . . . reminding and coaxing . . . nagging and bitching . . . judging and threatening . . . putting down and harping . . . hitting and pushing.

For example: A father was in the habit of waiting up for his daughter on Friday nights. Once she didn't arrive home until 2:30 in the morning — two hours after her curfew, with beer on her breath. She had driven her own car.

The father shouted, "Where in the hell have you been? It's 2:30 in the morning, and I've been waiting up for you all this time! And you've been drinking again! I can smell it over here! You'll never drive that car again, believe me! And you won't be going out for a while — for the rest of the year! So get to bed! I'm tired of you being so stupid!" Although he didn't hit his daughter, he almost did. Days later, when he told me the story, he was shaking.

Other Provoker behaviors include following the teenager around . . . reading diaries and journals . . . reading letters and listening in on phone calls . . . setting rules that are unreasonable and unrealistic . . . punishing without giving choices . . . choosing the teenager's friends.

For example: Whenever her son went out for the evening, a mother put on a wig, borrowed a neighbor's car, and followed him all around town. Sometimes she even looked in the windows of his friends' houses to see if he was using alcohol/drugs. The son told me later that he knew all along what she was doing, and would deliberately lead her on a wild-goose chase — going in the back door of a bar and out the front to make her think he was up to something.

Provokers tend to *over*react. They come down so hard, threaten so often, and get so close to physical abuse that they start to feel bad. At that point they back off and try to make amends. They become Rescuers.

- **Rescuers react out of guilt.**

We feel guilty when we overreact to our children's behaviors. We don't like to lose control. If we hit or hurt them, we immediately want to make amends by doing something nice for them. Many a teenager has suddenly acquired a new stereo, a bicycle, or even a car as a result of his or her parent's guilt feelings.

If we say things in anger that are difficult or impossible to enforce (like "You'll never go out again for the next 100 years!"), we will admit that we went too far and give in the next day with a far weaker warning ("All right, you can go out tonight, but don't let it happen again"). Many a teenager has avoided having to face the consequences for unacceptable behaviors as a result of his or her parent's guilt feelings.

Rescuer behaviors include being inconsistent with consequences . . . giving "one more chance" before effecting consequences . . . writing excuses for the school when a teenager has a hangover or oversleeps because of partying the night before . . . paying DWI or MIP fines . . . covering bounced checks . . . bailing the teenager out of jail . . . paying the costs of vandalism, stealing, or shoplifting . . . making excuses to relatives and friends for certain unacceptable behaviors on the part of the teenager, especially if they're connected to chemicals . . . repairing damages inflicted by the teenager at home or school . . . letting the teenager get away without doing his or her homework or other school assignments.

For example: A minister bailed his son out of jail six times for alcohol-related arrests. Each time the police called him, he paid the fine and brought his son home to save the congregation from embarrassment. It wasn't until the seventh arrest that he let his son sit in jail overnight — and even then he felt guilty.

And: A mother wrote an excuse to her daughter's school whenever her daughter was hungover or sick after a party. She wrote 53 excuses over a two-year period. Her daughter had the longest and most stubborn case of "stomach flu" in the school's history.

The Rescuer ends up doing things for the chemically dependent teenager. If the teenager takes advantage of this generosity by breaking the rules or behaving irresponsibly (coming in late, getting speeding tickets, or refusing to do chores), the Rescuer starts to feel like a fool — like someone who has been had. He or she then becomes a Victim.

- **Victims react out of hurt feelings.**

We can't understand it when our teenagers don't appreciate everything we have done for them. This is especially true when we have gone out of our way for months, maybe years, and all we've gotten in return has been sass talk, sign language (the raised middle finger), verbal abuse, and a blanket refusal to do chores or fulfill responsibilities around the house. We start feeling hurt. We start griping. We may even start to withdraw.

Victim behaviors include feeling sorry for oneself . . . complaining to one's spouse, neighbors, coworkers, and/or friends . . . feeling like a martyr . . . becoming more isolated from or fighting with one's spouse . . . becoming more isolated from one's friends and/or coworkers . . . putting more demands on other children in the family . . . comparing the teenager to other children . . . regretting that one ever had children . . . fantasizing about how good life would be without children . . . making plans to get even.

For example: A high-school junior was flunking school due to drinking and smoking marijuana. She usually came home late for dinner, at which point her father (a teacher in a local high school and a faithful churchgoer) would confront her on her tardiness and express his disappointment about her poor grades.

The girl would then say something like, "You know, Dad, I don't want to graduate. School isn't worth the trouble."

If that didn't hook her father's anger — she knew how much education meant to him — she would add something like, "You know, Dad, I've been thinking about becoming an atheist. Church is only for non-thinkers."

At this point her father would explode. Her mother would then come rushing into the room. She (the mother) was a recovering alcoholic and was still experiencing a lot of guilt from her drinking days. She would rescue her daughter from her husband's wrath. The young woman would go up to her room, hear her parents shouting at each other, and say to herself, "I won again."

Think of Provoker, Rescuer, and Victim as being the three sides on a triangle surrounding the chemically dependent teenager. An enabler can move from one position to another in days, hours, even minutes. The Victim can move from hurt to petulance and anger (the Provoker), then do something he or she feels awful about and move from anger to guilt (the Rescuer), then start resenting that role and become the Victim again. And so on, in any direction, *ad infinitum.*

When we see ourselves as responsible for others and start believing we can control their behaviors, feelings, and decisions, we automatically move into an enabling position.

Teenagers who use alcohol/drugs are pros at pushing the buttons that will get us to react. The chief buttons are anger, guilt, and hurt. If one doesn't work, another will.

Enabling comprises the third layer of the delusional system of chemical dependence in adolescents.

It's time to break through those layers.

Part II

INTERVENING WITH TEENAGERS IN TROUBLE WITH ALCOHOL/DRUGS

The object of intervention is to break through the delusional system in such a way that the chemically dependent person will accept the help he or she needs to arrest the disease and start recovering from it.

But intervention isn't just for the Level 4 teenager who is harmfully dependent on chemicals. It isn't just for the individual who has "hit bottom" and been expelled from school, kicked out of the house, arrested and jailed, or hospitalized after a suicide attempt. Intervention can "raise the bottom" for *any* teenager at *any* stage of the addiction process. In other words, *you don't have to wait until it seems too late.*

Successful intervention consists of three stages: *disengagement, confrontation,* and *reintegration.*

- Disengagement is the stage in which you *prepare* for intervention.
- Confrontation is the stage in which you *do* intervention.
- Reintegration is the stage in which you *follow up* intervention by helping the teenager to live without chemicals.

CHAPTER

CHAPTER

10

Disengagement: Preparing for Intervention

The first stage of intervention calls for you to break through the third layer of the delusional system and *stop enabling*. To put some space between you and the teenager's power plays. To BACK OFF.

For any power play to work, someone has to react to it. Your job right now is to disengage from this role so the power plays your teenager is using on you have nowhere to go. A power play without a target loses its power.

The theme for this stage is Take Care Of Yourself. This can be especially difficult for parents to do. We have been programmed to put our children first; anything else seems selfish. But if we really want to help our children, we must learn to put *ourselves first*.

Scripture teaches, "Love your neighbor as yourself." When we are busy enabling, we lose our ability to love ourselves. Our self-esteem suffers because we are trapped in a role doomed to failure: trying to control another person's behaviors, feelings, and decisions. Disengagement allows you to step out of this role and start shoring up your battered self-esteem.

There are three steps to disengagement: *getting support for yourself, forming a network of people willing to help,* and *learning ignoring skills.*

Step One: Getting Support for Yourself

This is something you can do right away. You don't have to wait for others to change their behaviors first. You can start *now*. Here's how:

1. Learn about the disease of chemical dependence and how it affects teenagers.

You have already begun by reading Part I of this book. You should have a basic understanding of the addiction process, the feeling disease, and what alcohol/drug use does to teenagers. If you want to know more, see pages 140-141 for a list of recommended reading materials and films.

2. Join a support group of parents with troubled teenagers.

Try a Families Anonymous or Al-Anon group.

Begun in 1971 by parents in southern California, Families Anonymous is a self-help program for families whose children exhibit destructive behaviors including alcohol/drug use, truancy, running away, dropping out, sexual promiscuity, and more. It is based on the Twelve Steps of Alcoholics Anonymous (A.A.) and Al-Anon — proven programs of recovery for chemically dependent people and their families. If you aren't familiar with the Twelve Steps, see page 142.

Both Families Anonymous and Al-Anon have chapters throughout the United States and Canada. Consult the White Pages of your local telephone directory to find a group near you. You'll meet other parents who are struggling with problems just like yours. You'll discover that *you are not alone.* You'll be accepted unconditionally, with no questions asked, and this will make it easier to start loving yourself.

By following the Twelve Steps, you'll get to know yourself better — your strengths, your weaknesses, your interests, your goals, your fears. You'll reclaim the feelings which have deadened over years of trying to control your children.

By attending Families Anonymous or Al-Anon meetings, you'll learn to accept the things you can't change and change the things you can — namely, yourself and your environment. And you will begin to laugh again.

Most parents of troubled teenagers have forgotten how to laugh, especially at themselves. It's usually fairly easy to pick out the new members of a Families Anonymous or Al-Anon group. They're the ones who are serious about everything and depressed most of the time. Those who are smiling have been attending for about three months. Those who are laughing at themselves have been there six months or more. It takes time, but laughter *does* come.

3. Make time for your own needs.

Start by sitting in a comfortable chair and just breathing. Do it slowly. Use your diaphragm, not only your chest. Experience the oxygen coming into your body as clean, clear, and life-giving. Experience the carbon dioxide going out as all the negative feelings (like guilt and failure) you've been carrying around for the past weeks, months, and maybe years.

Now close your eyes and feel the solidness of the chair you're sitting in. . .the floor the chair is sitting on. . .the foundation of the building. . .the rock upon which it was built. . .and the granite underneath the rock, going all the way to the center of the earth. Let your imagination carry you back up through the granite, the rock, the foundation, the floor, and the chair to a place of solidness *inside yourself*. Keep trying until you find it; you *will* find it. And you will know it as your "safe place" — somewhere you can always retreat to when things are going crazy around you.

- Set aside time each day for meditation. It might include prayer, scripture reading, reading poetry, listening to music, reading a good book, or just reflecting and relaxing your body.
- Practice relaxing your body. Start from the top of your head and move down through each muscle and bone to the tips of your toes. There are several audiotapes that can help you to do this. Check with your local bookstore.
- Take "minute vacations" throughout the day as needed. Pick some flowers; listen to the rain; watch a sunrise; look for rainbows; watch a sunset; gaze at the stars.
- Reexamine your expectations of yourself — as a parent, a spouse, a worker, a friend. Ask yourself how realistic they are, then lower them accordingly. Too often we parents set too-high goals for ourselves and our children.
- Ease up on your work; play more often. Get some exercise. Even something as simple as a daily walk can make a noticeable difference.
- Go out more. Make a date with your spouse or a friend. Leave town for a weekend. Remember — you're worth it!
- Put your problems in perspective. What difference will they make in a hundred years, or fifty, or even next year? The fact that your teenager is using alcohol/drugs doesn't signal the end of the world for you.
- Start really listening to others. What are they saying? What do they mean? Start listening to yourself. What is your body saying? What do *you* want and need?
- Take more time to do less. The enabling triangle is a tiring place to be. Provoking, rescuing, and being a victim consumes a lot of time and energy. When you do succeed in backing off from trying to control other people's behaviors, feelings, and decisions, you'll find yourself with extra time on your hands. Fill it with things *you* want to do.

4. Start gathering data on your teenager's behaviors.

Getting support for yourself also means determining that you haven't been imagining things — that your teenager really *does* have a problem and really *does* need help.

- Keep a daily journal of the troubling behaviors your teenager is exhibiting. Reread Chapters 6 and 7 to remind yourself of what to look for.

This information will prove important in three ways. First, it will help to convince you that you're not crazy. Second, it will help you to assess where your teenager is in the addiction process. And third, it will provide you with specific facts to present during the confrontation stage.

- Record behaviors you have observed *firsthand* that relate to your teenager's alcohol/drug use. Avoid rumors and hearsay; these can always be dismissed or denied.

To break through the layers of the delusional system, you will need to arm yourself with *objective facts* — not opinions, not judgments, but *facts*.

For example: One mother returned home from working the late shift to find her 17-year-old son and 16-year-old daughter passed out on the couch in front of the TV. They had gone to a pre-graduation beer party that evening. The daughter had gotten sick and thrown up all over the son's shirt.

First, the mother made sure that neither of her children was in danger of choking on his or her own vomit. Then she got her camera and took pictures. Then she took out her journal and described what she saw.

Later, during the confrontation stage, her children denied the incident as she described it. "Mom, you always exaggerate," her son insisted. "It wasn't that bad."

The mother replied, "Yes, it was that bad. I did not exaggerate. Look at these pictures."

• Make your descriptions as specific as possible. For each incident you record, note when it happened, where it happened, what was said, what was done, who else was there to witness it, and how you felt about it.

For example: One father wrote the following when his 16-year-old daughter came home drunk on a Saturday morning, three hours after her curfew.

> *You were brought home by your friends at 3:00 a.m. on December 10. They leaned you up against the door and rang the doorbell. When I opened the door, you fell into the porch and lay there. Your friends ran back to their van.*
>
> *I carried you into your room and put you to bed. I felt scared and hurt to see you like that.*
>
> *You got up at 8:30 a.m. to go to the bathroom. On your way out of your bedroom, you threw up all over our antique chair.*
>
> *You urinated in bed sometime during the night. I felt disgusted.*
>
> *You missed church on Sunday, December 11. You stayed in bed all day, complaining of nausea and a headache. I felt concerned because you were obviously ill.*
>
> *You missed school on Monday, December 12, claiming you were still sick. You also missed doing your chores. I felt angry.*

You can never be too specific when describing behaviors connected with your teenager's alcohol/drug use. The more detailed, the better.

Some parents have used tape recorders to capture the slurred speech, mumblings, or grandiose claims of their drunk or high teenagers. Some have even used video cameras. One mom and dad who arrived home from a vacation a day early walked into the scene of a party their son had thrown for his friends. More than 300 people had shown up at one time or another throughout the evening; everybody came when they heard there was a "parentless party" going on. Mom and Dad videotaped the whole mess.

5. Find out about resources in your community — places you can turn to for information, help, and support.

You'll probably be surprised at how much is available in your area.

- Start by making a list of crisis numbers and putting it near your telephone.

This should include emergency numbers (police, hospital emergency room, ambulance, your family physician) as well as the number of the local suicide hotline, detoxification center, treatment center, and juvenile court. Also list family members and friends you can count on to be there for you.

- Check the White Pages of your telephone directory for:
  — self-help groups (Alcoholics Anonymous, Narcotics Anonymous, Cocaine Anonymous, Families Anonymous, Al-Anon)
  — your county Social Services office
  — The Division of Alcoholism and Drug Abuse (you'll find this in either the Public Health Department or State Health Department or both)

- Check the Yellow Pages for:
  — Alcoholism Information and Treatment Centers
  — Drug Abuse Information and Treatment Centers
  — Mental Health Services
  — Human Services centers
  — Family Services organizations

- Contact national organizations for information on alcohol/drug abuse; self-help groups for addicts, family members, and parents; and alcohol/drug abuse prevention and education.

For a list of organizations, see pages 143-146.

6. Seek professional help.

You should *not* try to intervene by yourself. Successful intervention with teenagers requires a network of significant persons working closely together. It's too easy for a teenager to discount what one person has to say — and it's too easy for one person to fall back into enabling behaviors.

There are many experienced and capable professional caregivers who are ready and willing to assist you.

- Start with your teenager's school. More and more school personnel (teachers, counselors, administrators) are being trained in intervention techniques.
- Check out the juvenile court, out-patient and in-patient treatment centers, mental health clinics, county social services, recreational centers, and your church or temple.

Don't stop looking until you have found someone. Interview each "prospective" by finding out the following:

— Does he or she recognize chemical dependence as a disease?
— Does he or she support and believe in the intervention process?
— Has he or she had firsthand experience in intervening with teenagers?

The person who meets all three requirements is the person you want at your side as you continue through the next two stages of intervention.

Step Two: Forming a Network of People Willing to Help

Once you find a professional caregiver, you can begin to develop the rest of your network of significant persons.

The teenager impaired by delusion will usually find the weakest link in any network and will try to pit one part against another — whether at home (parent against parent), at school (teacher against administrator against counselor), or within the community (home against school against court against treatment). Remember that it takes a system to beat a system! Successful intervention requires that all parts work together to present a united front. The teenager must get the same message no matter where he or she goes: "You are responsible for your own behaviors. You have to experience your own pain and work through your own feelings. You sat on the burner, baby; you sit on the blisters."

To create this united front, work with the professional caregiver to:

1. Identify key persons around the teenager.

Who are the significant people in his or her life? Look to the immediate family (parents, siblings) and other relatives (grandparents, aunts and uncles). Does the teenager have any straight (non-using) friends who are concerned about his or her alcohol/drug use?

Who are the connectors — the "cookie people"? Look to the school (teachers, coaches, counselors, outreach workers), the legal system (police, probation officers, judges), your church or temple (ministers, priests, or rabbis, lay volunteers), and treatment centers (mental health professionals, counselors, group leaders).

Contact these key persons, explain the situation, and find

out if they are willing to help.

2. Set up a meeting of key persons you have identified and contacted.

This does not have to be a large group; five to seven people are usually enough. Try to get at least one representative from each agency the teenager is involved in (school, church or temple, legal). Friends can be important *as long as they are straight.*

Arrange to meet with the professional caregiver in his or her office (at the school, in the juvenile court, in a counseling agency, at a treatment center). Many schools today are developing policies for early intervention, evaluation, information groups, counseling, referral, and support groups for teenagers in trouble with alcohol/drugs.

Use this meeting to learn more about chemical dependence, share what you know about the teenager's alcohol/drug use, and explore various intervention, program, and treatment options. (The professional caregiver should be able to provide you with information on these.)

Step Three: Learning Ignoring Skills

Teenagers are pros at baiting their parents. We *mean* to keep our cool, we *mean* to keep our voices down, but a well-placed word or phrase from the mouth of a teenager can have us off and running before we know it.

It's not easy to disengage ourselves from these verbal power plays, but *it can be done.* We can learn to ignore them and not get hooked by them.

Author, counselor, teacher, and lecturer Tom Alibrandi has come up with five words and phrases you can use whenever your teenager starts playing verbal games. They're short, easy to remember, and amazingly effective. Here they are:

- "Yes."
- "No."
- "Oh, really?"
- "Wow."
- "Whatever."

These words and phrases can keep you out of the enabling triangle. Here's how they work:

Let's say you've set a 9:30 p.m. school-night curfew for your high school sophomore son. One night he asks, "Do I have to be in at 9:30 tonight?"

You answer, "Yes."

He presses it. "Can't I stay out until 10:30? Everybody else does!"

You answer, "No." At this point you might add, "That's the rule." Don't say it more than once, however; repetition constitutes nagging and provoking.

Now, if your son accepts the rule, he'll stop there. More than likely, though, he'll go on to test you to see if you really mean it.

Here's where the verbal games escalate into three distinct levels:

- First-degree verbal games: *Comparison Time*
- Second-degree verbal games: *Verbal Assault Time*
- Third-degree verbal games: *Go-For-The-Jugular Time*

Comparison Time goes something like this: "All the other parents let their kids stay out until 10:30! You're the only one who doesn't!"

The common parental response to this game is anger. You aren't like other parents, and you don't want to be like other parents. But instead of saying so, just answer, "Oh, really?" This will help keep you from being a Provoker.

Verbal Assault Time goes something like this: "This place sucks!"

The common parental response to this game is hurt feelings. Why can't your teenager appreciate all your years of hard work and sacrifice? But instead of giving a lecture, just answer, "Wow!" This will help keep you from being a Victim.

Go-For-The-Jugular Time goes something like this: "I'm going to do what I want, and you can't stop me. I'm going to stay out as long as I want. I might even get into some trouble. The police will pick me up and throw me in jail. You'll have to come down to the station to get me and then we'll have to go to court. It could even hit the newspapers. The neighbors will talk. Then you'll be sorry!"

The common parental response to this game is guilt. What did you do to cause your teenager to develop such an attitude? Where did you go wrong? You must have failed as a parent! But instead of pulling on your hair shirt, just answer, "Whatever." This will help keep you from being a Rescuer.

Repeat these little words and phrases to yourself: "Yes," "No," "Oh, really?", "Wow," "Whatever." Commit them to memory. Use them. They work!

Eight Tips to Help You Disengage

When you start disengaging from your role as enabler, your teenager can't help but notice. Up until now, he or she has been able to count on your Provoker, Victim, and Rescuer behaviors. Their sudden absence signals a change in your relationship that your teenager is bound to resist. He or she is liable to get VERY ANGRY WITH YOU.

1. Don't take that anger personally. It's like standing still while your teenager throws garbage at you. Instead, get out of the way and let it hit the wall!

You'll probably get angry in return; that's perfectly normal under the circumstances. BUT. . .

2. Don't confront your teenager when you're angry. Let him or her know how you feel, and explain that you need a cooling-off period. Set a time to talk later.

3. Avoid saying things you don't mean (like "I wish you had never been born!") or things you can't enforce ("You're grounded for 100 years!")

4. NEVER use violence, physical or verbal. Count to ten, count to 100, count to 1000 — whatever it takes.

Avoid falling into old enabling behavior patterns.

5. Don't nag your teenager or constantly remind him or her of the effects of alcohol/drug use. Take a stand, talk about your concerns, keep the lines of communication open, and express your feelings at appropriate times — but don't nag. Remember that nagging equals provoking, and provoking equals enabling.

6. Don't clean up your teenager's messes. Allow him or her to take responsibility for his or her own predicaments.
   — If your teenager is charged with MIP, don't pay the fine.
   — If he or she writes bad checks, don't cover them.
   — If your teenager breaks the law in other ways and ends up in jail overnight, let him or her stay there.
   — If his or her alcohol/drug use results in a car accident, don't pay for the repairs and higher insurance premiums.
   — If there is any loss or destruction of property, always require restitution.

7. Don't make excuses to family or friends about your teenager's alcohol/drug use. *Especially* don't write excuses to the school for hangovers or absences or tardiness.

Your teenager needs to experience the consequences of his or her own behaviors. Taking them on yourself equals rescuing, and rescuing equals enabling.

Finally:

8. Keep reminding yourself that chemical dependence is a disease. Your teenager isn't weak, lacking in will power, or a failure as a person; your teenager is sick. And *it is not your fault*. Repeat this until you believe it; it's true.

11

The Professional's Role in Disengagement

If you are asked to help with intervention, the first group meeting is your opportunity to gather information about and from the key people involved.

- *Determine how much they know about the disease of chemical dependence.*

To function effectively in intervention, they should have some understanding of the disease, its characteristics, the four phases (use, misuse, abuse, and addiction), and the delusional system that accompanies it. They need to know that the teenager will probably die prematurely if he or she continues to use alcohol/drugs; that the teenager can't stop using them on his or her own; and that the delusional system prevents the teenager from recognizing that he or she has the disease. They also need to understand what enabling is and how easy it is for them to act as enablers.

You may use the meeting as a teaching session. Or, if you prefer, have group members review Chapters 1-9 of this book or attend informational classes on chemical dependence.

- *Evaluate their degree of enabling and their emotional capacity to disengage.*

The question to ask yourself is, "Are these people emotionally prepared to be interveners?" Some may be reluctant to confront the teenager out of fear that they will jeopardize their relationship or friendship with him or her. Watch for those who make excuses or exhibit Rescuer behaviors.

Others may be incapable of confronting without anger. Watch for any tendency toward Provoker behaviors. Still others may be too wrapped up in their own hurt feelings. Watch for Victim behaviors.

Clarify to the group the difference between enabling (being responsible for) and caring (being responsible to). Many people are able to work through their fear, anger, and personal pain when they realize that the teenager desperately needs their help. If it becomes clear that one or more cannot, it's better that they not take part in intervention until or unless they are able to disengage.

• *Gather data about the teenager's alcohol/drug use.*

Have group members make written lists of specific incidents related to the alcohol/drug use. Stress that this must be *firsthand* knowledge of incidents and behaviors. Gossip and secondhand information should be avoided, along with generalities like "I think he (or she) is drinking too much."

Also have group members identify the feelings they have when these behaviors occur. For example: "It hurts me/scares me/embarrasses me when. . . ."

Initially, this data will help you to determine the teenager's level of usage. Later, it will help you to decide what kind of intervention to do.

There are additional kinds of information you will need to gather from other sources. Specifically:

— Has the teenager broken any laws? Find out from the juvenile court.
— Has the teenager's school performance changed noticeably? When a teenager gets into trouble with alcohol/

drugs, this usually shows up first at school. Ask the school to furnish you with report cards, attendance records (look for evidence of increased absences or tardiness), and information on the teenager's extracurricular activities. Find out from teachers how the teenager has been behaving in class.

Some schools are now using behavioral checklists to solicit input from staff members involved with teenagers who are using alcohol/drugs. See page 147 for an example.

- *Be prepared to introduce, explain, and discuss the available intervention, treatment, and other program options.*

These will depend on local laws, school policies and procedures, and on what your area offers. They might include first-phase information groups and second-phase intervention groups in the school, court, or human services setting.

Topics covered in a *first-phase information group* include:

— why each person is in the group
— reasons for using chemicals
— types of drugs and their effects on the user
— levels of usage (an introduction to the disease concept of chemical dependence)
— types of chemicals used by participants and the frequency of use
— role-plays (school scenes, court scenes)
— communication skills (group members give feedback to one another)
— possible alternatives to chemicals
— myths about alcoholism and other drug addiction

Topics covered in a *second-phase intervention group* include:

— why each person is in the group

— the disease concept of chemical dependence (the addiction process, the feeling disease)
— self-evaluations and interviews
— role-plays (defenses; enabling)
— identification of memory distortions
— personal stories shared by recovering persons
— available treatment and self-help programs

If it appears that the teenager will require some form of treatment, find out the following:

— What is the school's policy on chemical abuse?
— What is the police department's policy for dealing with teenagers arrested for breaking alcohol/drug laws?
— What are the juvenile court's procedures for committing teenagers to treatment for chemical dependence?
— How and under what circumstances does the detoxification center perform alcohol/drug evaluations?

Be ready to outline the available treatment options. These might include in-patient and out-patient programs, detoxification centers, and self-help programs such as Alcoholics Anonymous (A.A.), Narcotics Anonymous (N.A.), Cocaine Anonymous (C.A.), and Alateen for teenage chemical dependents who also have chemically dependent parents and/or siblings.

When discussing treatment programs, you should know what they involve, how much they cost, how long they take, what provisions they make for family involvement and aftercare, and which self-help, Twelve-Step-based groups they support and encourage participants to attend. The more you can tell group members (especially parents), the more secure they will feel about intervention.

If you are experienced in intervening with adults, you should know that intervening with teenagers is different in a number of important ways. Specifically:

Intervention with adults usually involves family members and employers; intervention with teenagers usually involves more "outside" people.

You may not be able to count on the parents' support. A large percentage of young people in trouble with alcohol/ drugs have a chemically dependent parent. The parents may be so involved with their own problems that they simply can't help.

Some are rendered so psychologically and emotionally dysfunctional by their relationship with the chemically dependent person that they can't stop enabling long enough to help. They are *co-dependent** and are as deluded about addiction as the chemical dependent himself or herself.

We cannot wait for parents to recover before intervening with teenagers. We can, however, turn to the school, the court, and treatment centers for the people we need. Because chemical use has legal implications for adolescents, it's possible for the school or the court to require that intervention be done with or without the parents' involvement.

Intervention with adults may require one session, or several; intervention with teenagers always requires more than one session.

Intervention with teenagers involves a series of contracts or agreements, starting with the least restrictive and moving toward the most restrictive. Teens must be actively and routinely involved with agreed-upon behaviors and they need to be regularly confronted with evidence from contracts that state these behaviors. These are explained in Chapter 12.

---

*If you are not familiar with the term *co-dependent*, read *Diagnosing and Treating Co-Dependence: A Guide for Professionals Who Work with Chemical Dependents, Their Spouses, and Children* by Timmen L. Cermak, M.D. (Minneapolis: Johnson Institute, 1986).

Intervention with adults makes use of existing contracts; intervention with teenagers makes use of contracts developed especially for that purpose.

Adults have marriage and employment contracts that can be put on the line during intervention. (For example, a spouse can say, "If you don't agree to treatment, I will take the children and move out." Or an employer can say, "If you don't agree to treatment, you will no longer have a job.")

But most teenagers aren't married and don't have jobs (at least, not permanent ones), so these contracts don't exist for them. Special contracts must be developed for intervention purposes. These are explained in Chapter 12.

Intervention with teenagers requires a more extensive network of significant persons than intervention with adults.

Intervention with adults usually involves the family, a boss, a friend, and maybe the court. Intervention with teenagers may involve the family, the school, the court, a treatment center, the church or temple, a hospital, a recreation center, and friends.

There are more support and aftercare programs for adults than for teenagers.

Adults coming out of treatment are encouraged to attend A.A. meetings and weekly support groups. Teenagers are encouraged to attend similar groups. But where do we send them after treatment? Back to school — and back to their using friends.

There is a pressing need for more support and aftercare programs in the school setting; for Alcoholics Anonymous, Narcotics Anonymous and Cocaine Anonymous groups for teenagers; for aftercare groups in treatment programs; for non-chemical recreational activities; and for recovering teenagers who can serve as models for peers who have just gone through intervention. Unfortunately, many communities don't yet have such resources.

As a result, we must rely on intervention itself to do the job. That is one reason why intervention with teenagers always requires more than one session and is more of an ongoing process than intervention with adults.

Teenagers require different treatment modalities than adults.

Adults usually respond to "therapy groups," A.A. groups, and the like. Teenagers need more experiential groups that include assertiveness training and self-esteem-building classes. They also need recreational and occupational therapy, tutoring in school subjects, and help in dealing with sexuality issues, grief issues, and children-of-alcoholics issues. In short, teenagers need more help in developing life skills.

Adult children of alcoholics who undergo treatment are encouraged to wait for six months to a year before tackling grief issues stemming from their childhoods. If they were sexually abused as children, an even longer period of sobriety is recommended before starting to work on those issues.

Adults can afford to take their time because these are generally issues that relate to the past. For teenagers with alcoholic and/or abusive parents, these issues are very much in the present and cannot be set aside to be dealt with later. Support groups are essential during treatment, and child protection services must often be brought into the circle.

CHAPTER

12

Confrontation: Doing Intervention

The second stage of intervention calls for you to break through the second and first layers of the delusional system — the memory distortions and rigid defenses — *and present reality to your teenager in a receivable way*. To help him or her accept that reality by SETTING LIMITS. To control the environments — home and school — where your teenager spends most of his or her time.

Your job right now is to work with the other key people you have identified to let the teenager know that you're dead serious. If your teenager is chemically dependent, setting limits will give him or her the sense of security he or she has lost to alcohol/drugs.

The theme for this stage is Take Back Your Environment. Teenagers on alcohol/drugs tend to control the environments they live in. Parents feel like prisoners in their own homes. Teachers feel trapped in their own classrooms. Confrontation allows you to regain the control you have lost.

Before teenagers can accept the reality of how alcohol/drugs are affecting them, *they must be straight* — they must stop using mood-altering chemicals. Getting them to stop isn't easy. This is why the united front is so important. Significant persons in a teenager's life must work together to send this message:

"Chemicals have affected your living at home, your progress at school, and your behavior in the community. They have affected you at all levels of your life: physical, mental, emotional, and spiritual. Since we cannot control your decision to use or not to use, we will control the environment by setting limits. Your behavior will tell us what limits to set. These limits will protect you while you regain control over your own life."

Of course the teenager will resist your efforts. He or she will test your limits and your patience and push your buttons constantly. You will be sorely tempted to start enabling again, which is why it is critical for you *not* to attempt confrontation alone. You will need the support of other concerned persons, and you will need the help of a professional caregiver.

There are three steps to confrontation: *learning the "4 C's" of confrontation, using them,* and *learning confrontation skills.*

Step One: Learning the "4 C's" of Confrontation

There are four essential parts to confrontation: *choices, consequences, contracts,* and *control.*

1. Choices

Confrontation is not punishment. It does not use violence, threats, shouting, judging, moralizing, or humiliation. It is based on respect and done in such a way that the teenager can receive the information you are presenting without losing face or feeling put down. It elicits the teenager's cooperation and involvement in the intervention process.

Never put a teenager in a corner without a way out. Always be prepared to offer choices. This gives the teenager a sense of dignity and control over his or her life. Remember that all teenagers — and especially chemically dependent teenagers — have enough problems with low-self esteem without your compounding them!

There are three situations in which you should be prepared to offer choices to your teenager.

• *When you are addressing a specific behavior.*

Your teenager is watching TV and hasn't done his homework. You say, "You can do your homework now and be free to go out after dinner, or you can wait until after we eat and stay in to do it. What do you want to do?"

• *When you are determining consequences.*

Your teenager breaks curfew by two hours. You say, "You have to come in two hours earlier next Friday night, or stay in for the next two nights. What do you want to do?"

• *When you are enforcing consequences.*

Your teenager is caught with drugs at home, and your spouse doesn't know it yet. You say, "I can tell your father (or mother), or you can. How do you want to do it?"

2. Consequences

Although confrontation is not punishment, this doesn't mean it's permissive. Instead, it involves well-defined rules and consequences for breaking those rules.

Rules set limits and perimeters to a teenager's environment. An effective rule is *specific* ("Your curfew on weeknights is 9:30"), *reasonable* ("That gives you time to spend with your friends and also get enough sleep"), and *enforceable* (it's your home).

Apply the same three criteria to rules about alcohol/drug use. Make them *specific* ("NO USE whatsoever"), *reasonable* ("It's against the law"), and *enforceable* (again, it's your home).

Consequences can be either *natural* or *logical*. Natural consequences are those that happen on their own, with no action on your part. Events are simply allowed to run their course. For example: getting wet when you stand in the rain, getting cold when you forget your coat, getting hungry when you don't eat. For teenagers who use chemicals, a natural consequence might be a hangover. (With some teenagers, natural consequences for using chemicals could also include overdosing, violent acts, or suicide attempts. In these cases, you will need to take direct action.)

Logical consequences require some action on your part to help the teenager experience the full impact of his or her behavior. An effective logical consequence is *related* to the incident ("You were drinking in your car, so I'm going to take your keys away"), *reasonable* ("I'm going to keep them for a month"), and *set up in advance* with the teenager's knowledge ("We agreed earlier that if you drank in your car, you'd lose your keys for a month, so what I'm doing now is holding you to that agreement.") They must also be enforced calmly, with respect, and without anger.

Your professional caregiver can help you to determine other logical consequences. In addition, some may be set up by the school or the court. These might include:

- detention in school for skipping classes,
- suspension from school for alcohol/drug possession,
- spending time in jail for DUI, illegal acts, or violent acts,
- required evaluations or attendance at information sessions about the effects of chemicals.

3. Contracts

Confrontation isn't "snoopervision." It doesn't involve smelling your teenager's breath whenever he or she comes home, doing urine analyses, opening lockers to look for alcohol/drugs, searching bedrooms, reading diaries, or listening in on phone conversations. These actions are required only in extreme cases — such as when a teenager is exhibiting suicidal tendencies.

Rather, confrontation involves the *supervision* and monitoring of behaviors at home, at school, and in the community. These behaviors are set out clearly in contracts drawn up with the teenager. So, too, are the consequences for not abiding by those behaviors.

Contracts perform a number of important functions:
— They help teenagers take responsibility for themselves.
— They give them some control over their environment.
— They help them to make choices — the consequences include choices.
— They help them to develop trust — the consequences are always consistent.
— They let them know in advance what will happen if they break the rules — the consequences are spelled out ahead of time.
— They allow teenagers to prove that they are not chemically dependent — by abiding by the rules.
— They help to determine when a teenager should be placed in another environment.

There are three types of contracts that can be used in the confrontation stage:

• *The Simple Contract*

This is a written agreement that includes basic non-negotiable rules: no alcohol or other drug use, no violence (physical or verbal), and no skipping of classes or information group sessions.

Consequences for breaking this contract include the choice between a chemical dependence *evaluation* in an out-patient setting, or one in an in-patient setting.

- *The Turf Contract*

This is a written agreement that includes all the rules of the Simple Contract and outlines specific behaviors required for the teenager to earn certain privileges at home (curfews, use of the car or telephone) or at school (participation in activities or sports). These behaviors might include negotiable tasks regarding school performance, personal cleanliness, curfew hours, and chores at home.

Consequences for breaking this contract include the choice between treatment in an out-patient setting, or in an in-patient setting.

- *The Bottom-Line Contract*

This is a written agreement that outlines specific behaviors required for the teenager to retain the privileges of living at home and staying in school. They may include all the elements of both the Simple Contract and the Turf Contract.

Consequences for breaking this contract include the choice between two available and reputable in-patient treatment centers.

4. Control

By setting rules, determining consequences, and spelling them all out in contracts, you are Taking Back Your Environment. You are re-establishing your control over what goes on in it. You are *not* controlling your teenager's behaviors, feelings, and decisions. You *are* saying, in effect, "If you choose to break the rules of the contract, this is how I will change the environment."

How you change the environment depends on the teenager's needs, which are evidenced in his or her behaviors. These may indicate a need for an educational program, an evaluation, out-patient treatment, or in-patient treatment. In some cases it may become necessary to change the environment immediately — calling an ambulance for a teenager who has overdosed, calling the police for a teenager who has become violent, calling a mental health worker or a psychiatrist for a teenager who is suicidal.

It may also become necessary to remove the teenager from the home or school to a more protective environment for a period of time. This isn't the same as abandoning the teenager or turning your back on him or her; rather, it's another way of being responsible to the teenager who can no longer be responsible for himself or herself.

Step Two: Using the "4 C's" of Confrontation

The confrontation stage of intervening with teenagers takes time. It will probably take at least two sessions and maybe more before you can break through the second and first layers of the delusional system.

You won't get a teenager to "receive reality" by confronting him or her with facts you have written on a list or by just sharing your feelings and concerns. Instead, you must remind the teenager that he or she has not behaved according to mutually agreed upon rules of behavior, and that mutually agreed upon consequences will now take effect because those rules of behavior were not followed.

The movement in the confrontation stage is from the *least restrictive agreement* (the verbal "No Use" agreement) through *more restrictive* agreements (the Simple Contract, the Turf Contract) to the *most restrictive agreement* (the Bottom-Line contract).

The teenager's ability to abide by these agreements will tell you what level of usage he or she is at and how much more help he or she needs.

You don't have to label your teenager or judge whether he or she is chemically dependent. That's not your job. It's up to the teenager to show that he or she *isn't* by living according to the terms of the agreements you work out together. That's the teenager's responsibility. Yours is to control yourself and your environment by setting limits.

There are four levels of confrontation. These correspond to the phases of the feeling disease among teenagers: learning the mood swing, seeking the mood swing, harmful involvement, and harmful dependence. Recall that in the first three phases, the teenager can still choose to use or not. In the fourth phase the teenager has lost control and choice.

Level 1 (for teenagers learning the mood swing): The "No Use" Rule

If you discover that your teenager is using alcohol/drugs, you should immediately set up a "No Use" rule.

We are not talking here about acceptable use at a meal, in the liturgy, or for medical reasons. We are referring to experimental and other use outside the home, or inside the home without your knowledge. As soon as you learn that this is going on, you need to take a stand.

In setting up your "No Use" rule, simply follow the guidelines established by your community and your teenager's school. These usually include the following:

— no drinking alcohol if under the legal age limit (21, in most states)
— no possession or use of illegal drugs
— no illegal actions related to alcohol/drug use — specifically, no drinking or using other drugs while driving; no open containers or drug paraphernalia in the car

To make your "No Use" rule effective, it must have conse-

quences. Keep them simple and clear, and spell them out in
advance. These might include:

— enforcing school regulations established by your State
Activity Association (generally speaking, if a teenager
is caught using alcohol/drugs, he or she is barred from
participating in school activities)
— letting your teenager spend the night in jail if arrested
and charged with a DWI or DUI

One father discovered that his son, the star quarterback on
the high-school football team, had been smoking marijuana.
He immediately set up a "No Use" rule with this consequence: If he learned that his son was using marijuana at any
time, he would call the school and tell them.

On the Saturday night before the week of the playoff game,
the son came home high from a party. On Monday morning,
the father called the school. The school officials suspended
the son from playing for the rest of the season. The team lost
the playoff game by one touchdown.

Several parents blamed the father for the loss. He re-
sponded that it was his son's choice to break the "No Use"
rule, not his.

Another father let his son spend the night in jail when he
was arrested for driving while intoxicated. Prior to the arrest,
he had told all of his children that if they ever ended up in jail
for breaking the law, they should call him and let him know
where they were. "But if you're smart enough to get into
jail," he informed them, "you're smart enough to get out."

In both cases, the parents enforced the consequences already set up by the school and the court.

You may want to add your own consequences. For example, use natural consequences if your teenager has a hangover: no sympathy, and no excuses if he or she misses a day of
school. Logical consequences might include an earlier curfew,

curtailed telephone or car privileges, or attendance at an information group about chemical dependence. Don't forget to build choices into your consequences, and be sure to set up the consequences in advance with your teenager's knowledge.

Here's an example of how you might use the first level of confrontation to control your environment:

Your 16-year-old son, John, comes home from a dance obviously intoxicated. This is the second time you have seen him drunk. The first time he had "a couple of beers" with his friends, you set up a "No Use" rule and outlined specific consequences. John has now broken this rule. He wasn't driving a car, and the dance wasn't a school function.

Start by checking to see if he is in crisis. Is he violent? Is he suicidal? Is he high on other drugs, too? Is there a chance of an overdose? If the answer to any of these questions is "yes," get him to the proper place for emergency care. If the answer to all of these questions is "no," then do the following:

— Let him sleep where he falls. Don't caretake, and don't confront when he's still under the influence.

— Talk to him in the morning — unless you're still angry. If that's the case, wait. Don't confront while angry.

— Express your concern about his behavior. "John, I feel very concerned when you come home drunk. You could have gotten into serious trouble with the law, or you could have gotten hurt."

— Repeat your "No Use" rule and its consequences, then give him a choice between those consequences. "John, you know the consequences for drinking or using other drugs. You will be suspended from all activities for three weeks. If you go to a class about chemical dependence, you can reduce that to one week. What do you want to do?"

— After John makes his choice, monitor his behavior to

learn if he sticks to it. If he abides by the "No Use" rule, he is telling you that he is still in control and can choose to use or not. If he continues to use, he is telling you that it's time to move to the second level of confrontation and the Simple Contract.

Level 2 (for teenagers seeking the mood swing): The Simple Contract

A teenager at Level 2 (misuse) has been using alcohol/ drugs with some regularity. He or she has been breaking the law. Schoolwork has been affected. The teenager may have been arrested for using at a party or in a car and charged with Minor In Possession, or he or she may have been caught coming to a school function intoxicated or high. In either case, you have been notified.

Consequences for breaking the law might include jail time and probation. Consequences for breaking school rules might include suspension from activities and maybe even school itself. Both require attendance at a first-phase information group on chemical dependence run either by the school or the court (but usually held at the school). At this level, the teenager is put on a Simple Contract.

The Simple Contract, as explained earlier, is a written agreement with non-negotiable rules including no chemical use, no violence, and no skipping of information group meetings.

The consequences for breaking any of these rules include an evaluation by a chemical dependence counselor, attendance at a second-phase intervention group held at school, court, or a human service setting, and a Turf Contract. The teenager is given the choice of where to go for the evaluation — either an out-patient program or an in-patient program.

Here's an example of how you might use the second level of

confrontation to control your environment:

Your daughter, Susie, is caught drinking with her boyfriend at a school dance. She is held in the principal's office, and you are called to pick her up.

You arrive at the school very angry. Earlier you had talked with Susie about the "No Use" rule, and she had insisted that you didn't have anything to worry about. "Kids who drink and use drugs are stupid," she had told you. Susie is a good athlete (she's on the basketball team) and an above-average student (B's and A's). She has come home intoxicated only one time, but that was before you set up the "No Use" rule.

Now you listen to the teacher who caught her with the alcohol. Then you see if Susie has anything to say. You ask the teacher what the consequences are for breaking the school regulation on drinking. You learn that you need to come to school on Monday to meet with the principal, who will offer the choice of a one-day or three-day suspension. For Susie to qualify for the one-day suspension, she must agree to attend a first-phase information group. A Simple Contract will be required regardless of her choice.

You take Susie home and talk to her the next day about breaking the "No Use" rule. You tell her that she has lost her telephone privileges and use of the car for the weekend. You *don't* nag or shout. When you explain the choices she will be offered on Monday, she decides to take the one-day suspension with information group attendance.

On Monday, you meet with the principal, who explains the suspension policy. He also informs you that Susie will be suspended from playing basketball for two weeks. An appointment is set up with the counselor who runs the information group.

You and Susie both meet with the counselor, who explains the terms of the Simple Contract: no use of chemicals, no violence, and attendance at information group. Susie signs the contract, and you witness it.

Then you monitor her behavior *at home* to see whether she is abiding by the terms of the contract. You don't threaten, interrogate, or "snoopervise." Instead, you give Susie your support, express your concerns, and repeat the "No Use" rule — once.

Meanwhile, the counselor monitors Susie's behavior at school. You and the counselor stay in contact, reporting any use of chemicals, acts of violence, or skipping of information group sessions.

If Susie sticks to the terms of the contract, she is telling you that she is still in control and can choose to use or not. If she breaks *any* of the rules in the contract, she is telling you that it's time to move to the third level of confrontation and the Turf Contract.

SAMPLE SIMPLE CONTRACT

I agree to the following terms:

1) No chemical use (this includes alcohol and other drugs)
2) No violence (verbal or physical, inside or outside the information group)
3) No skipping information group sessions (this means attendance at ALL unless excused ahead of time by the group leader)

Privileges:
Use of the telephone and use of the car (suspended for the first weekend — 2 days)
Hours (regular after the first week)

Consequences:
If *any* of the above conditions are not kept, then the following will happen:

1) Evaluation by a CD counselor (out-patient or in-patient)
2) Attendance at a second-phase intervention group
3) Put on Turf Contract

Signature:_____ Date:_____
   (Teenager)
Witness:_____ Date:_____
   (Parent)

Length of contract:_____ weeks or until the group is finished.

Level 3 (for teenagers who are harmfully involved): The Turf Contract

A teenager at Level 3 (abuse) is preoccupied with alcohol/drugs. More laws have probably been broken, truancy has increased, grades have dropped, curfew has been violated repeatedly, and most friends are alcohol/drug using friends. The teenager is very defensive when confronted. It is necessary to move on to a more restrictive environment.

The consequences of not keeping the Simple Contract include an evaluation by a chemical dependence counselor, attendance at a second-phase intervention group, and a Turf Contract.

The Turf Contract, as explained earlier, is a written agreement that includes all the non-negotiable rules of the Simple Contract. It also outlines specific behaviors required for the teenager to earn certain privileges at home (curfews, use of the car or telephone) or at school (participation in activities or sports).

The consequences for breaking any of the terms of this contract include treatment for chemical dependence, individual counseling, and a Bottom-Line Contract. The teenager is given the choice between treatment in an out-patient setting or treatment in an in-patient setting.

Here's an example of how you might use the Turf Contract to control your environment:

Your son, Tom, is caught snorting cocaine at a wrestling meet. Because he is in possession of an illegal substance, the school calls the police, who take him to the detention center. You are called to pick him up.

This isn't his first drug-related offense. Three months earlier, he was charged with a Minor in Possession and attended a first-phase information group at his school as part of his probation. You decide to let him spend the night at the center.

When you pick him up the next day, he is furious with you for leaving him there overnight and defensive about getting arrested. He blames the school for being "out to get him"; he rationalizes that "a bunch of kids were doing coke," including some of the wrestlers; he minimizes that he only did "a couple of lines"; and he denies that the cocaine was his, insisting that someone had given it to him and he "didn't want to be a square."

You remind yourself not to take Tom's anger personally — he is projecting his own pain on you to avoid dealing with it himself. Then you tell Tom that you will be talking to his probation officer.

Upon meeting with the probation officer, you learn that since Tom violated his probation, he is required to have an evaluation by a chemical dependence counselor. You and the probation officer give Tom the choice between having the evaluation done in an out-patient or an in-patient setting. He chooses the out-patient setting.

You, the school, and the court will all provide information to assist with the evaluation. This data will come from your personal journal of Tom's alcohol/drug-related behaviors, school checklists, and court records.

The probation officer then tells Tom that he will have to attend a second-phase intervention group at the school and be put on a Turf Contract. This contract can be written either by the probation officer, or by the group counselor at the school.

You and Tom both meet with the probation officer or the counselor, who explains the terms of the contract: the non-negotiable behaviors of the Simple Contract (no use, no violence, no skipping intervention group), and negotiable behaviors such as curfew hours, chores at home, and school performance. The contract also spells out certain privileges Tom must earn by keeping to the terms of the contract. Points are assigned to each behavior and determine whether privileges are granted or not. Tom and you sign the contract, and the probation officer or counselor witnesses it.

Importantly, the granting of privileges depends on the total contract, not on any one behavior. Tom either makes enough points to earn the privileges or makes too few and doesn't earn them. *There are no exceptions* or "special occasions" allowed. However, it is unrealistic to expect 100 percent perfect performance. We recommend using 90 percent as a guide.

Unlike the Simple Contract, the Turf Contract also includes a renegotiation date, at which time the consequences and privileges are reviewed. This allows everyone to save face, especially if changes are called for.

If Tom objects to the contract, insisting that he is *not* "hooked" on drugs, you respond, "It's not our job to prove that you are. It's your responsibility to show that you aren't. Just keep the contract; if you can't, this will show us that you're out of control and need more help."

If Tom sticks to the terms of the contract, he is telling you that he is still in control and can choose to use or not. If he doesn't keep it, he is telling you that it's time to move to the fourth level of confrontation and the Bottom-Line Contract.

SAMPLE TURF CONTRACT

For_____ Week of_____ through_____
          Name   Date   Date

BEHAVIOR/TASK	POSSIBLE POINTS	S	M	T	W	TH	F	S	TOTAL
Keeping curfews									
10:00 weeknight	10	X	X	X	X	X			/50
12:30 weekend (one night or two)	10						X	X	/20
No drunk or high behavior (stumbling, staggering, swearing, slurring) or drug paraphernalia	10	X	X	X	X	X	X	X	/70
No violence (physical or verbal)	10	X	X	X	X	X	X	X	/70
School attendance (all classes)	10		X	X	X	X	X		/50
Chores at home (dishes M, W, F garbage T, Th, Sat)	5		X	X	X	X	X	X	/30
2nd-phase intervention group attendance	10				X				/10

TOTAL POINTS POSSIBLE   300
TOTAL POINTS EARNED   _____

PRIVILEGES/POINTS NEEDED

Telephone, week nights out: 270 points (90%)
Car, 1 night out on weekend: 285 points (95%)
2 nights out on weekend: 300 points (100%)
All are suspended for first week, then can be earned by making points.

Consequences if 80% not maintained:

1) Treatment (out-patient or in-patient)
2) Counseling and continue with 2nd-phase intervention group
3) Bottom-Line Contract with loss of privileges for 2 weeks

Signed:_____Date_____
          (Teenager)

Signed:_____Date_____
          (Parent)

Witness:_____Date_____
          (Probation officer or counselor)

Renegotiation Date:_____

Level 4 (for teenagers who are harmfully dependent):
The Bottom-Line Contract

At this level of usage, the teenager has lost both control and choice. The use of alcohol/drugs has become compulsive. The chemicals have become primary in his or her life. The symptoms are progressive and chronic. Without intervention, the teenager will probably die prematurely. The disease of chemical dependence is fatal, and many teenagers have died from it.

Many people believe that before a chemical dependent can start recovering, he or she must first "hit bottom." But what does it mean to "hit bottom"? And where does this happen?

Here are some examples drawn from actual case histories.

In jail: Teenage chemical dependents often commit crimes such as robbery, dealing drugs, assault and battery, and vandalism. One boy ended up in prison at age 17. He entered a treatment program there and is presently straight.

At school: One 17-year-old girl came to school drunk and wrecked the principal's office when she was brought there by her teachers. The police were called in and had to restrain her with handcuffs. She was then taken to jail, where she tried (and failed) to take her own life. After being assigned to a psychiatric unit, she was evaluated as being chemically dependent, went to treatment, and is straight today.

At home: One 18-year-old boy beat up his mother while in a blackout. When his father came home, he attacked him too. His parents called the police and had him arrested. He was evaluated while in jail and sent to treatment. He returned to treatment twice; he is sober today.

On the streets: One 16-year-old boy built explosive devices in the basement of his home while high on drugs. His desperate parents ordered him to leave. On the streets, he ran into an old friend who had stopped using and joined Narcotics

Anonymous. The friend took him to a meeting, and from there he went to treatment. He is straight today.

In a hospital: One 15-year-old boy overdosed on PCP ("angel dust") and was brought to the emergency room and immediately placed in intensive care. After two weeks, he was evaluated and sent to treatment. He returned three times before finally staying straight.

On a psychiatric unit: One 16-year-old girl went wild in a park while tripping on LSD ("acid"). She was arrested and placed on a psychiatric unit for three months. She went into treatment and returned four times before finding sobriety.

All of these teenagers were suicidal before getting help. Yet they were the lucky ones — because someone intervened. Many more have not found sobriety. They are still using, or they are dead.

We don't have to wait until a teenager nearly dies from alcohol/drug use. We don't have to wait until he or she hits bottom before doing something. We can "raise the bottom" through intervention.

For Level 4 teenagers, intervention involves a Bottom-Line Contract. As explained earlier, the Bottom-Line Contract is a written agreement that outlines specific behaviors required for the teenager to retain the privileges of living at home and staying in school. These may include all the non-negotiable items of the Simple Contract and the negotiable items of the Turf Contract.

Like the Turf Contract, the Bottom-Line Contract is based on a points system. To retain the privileges of living at home and staying in school, the teenager must earn 90% of the total points possible per week over a two-week period. All other privileges are suspended during this time.

Input from all of the agencies the teenager is involved with will be used in putting this contract together. As many as four or five different agencies may be represented, including the school, the court, a recreational center, and a treatment center — as well as the home. Once the contract has been signed, the parents monitor the teenager's behavior daily and the professional caregiver reviews the contract every week.

If the Bottom-Line Contract is kept, the teenager then goes back to the Turf Contract, where he or she can start earning the privileges that were suspended with the Bottom-Line Contract. You determine the length of time for this contract, based on how responsibly the teenager behaves.

Consequences for breaking the Bottom-Line Contract include the choice between two available and reputable in-patient treatment centers. Note that the choice isn't one of *whether* the teenager will go into treatment, but *where*.

SAMPLE BOTTOM-LINE CONTRACT

For_____ Week of_____ through_____
            Name   Date   Date

BEHAVIOR/TASK	POSSIBLE POINTS	S	M	T	W	TH	F	S	TOTAL
Keeping curfews									
Stay home after 6 p.m. on weeknights	10	X	X	X	X	X			/50
Stay home after 6 p.m. on weekend nights	10						X	X	/20
No drunk or high behavior (stumbling, staggering, swearing, slurring) or drug paraphernalia	10	X	X	X	X	X	X	X	/70
No violence (physical or verbal)	10	X	X	X	X	X	X	X	/70
School attendance (all classes)	10		X	X	X	X	X		/50
Chores at home (dishes M, W, F garbage T, Th, Sat)	5		X	X	X	X	X	X	/30
2nd-phase intervention group attendance	10		X						/10
See probation officer	10				X				/10
See out-patient counselor	10		X						/10

TOTAL POINTS POSSIBLE   320
TOTAL POINTS EARNED   ____

PRIVILEGES/POINTS NEEDED

    Living at home: 288 points (90%) each week are necessary over a two-week period of time. All other privileges are lost for duration of contract. If 90% is achieved for two weeks, then move back to Turf Contract to regain privileges.

Consequences if 90% not achieved: In-patient treatment at an available and reputable treatment center. Not allowed at home until treatment is completed.

Signed:_____Date_____
        (Teenager)

      _____Date_____
        (Parent)

Witness:_____Date_____
        (Probation officer or counselor)

Renegotiation Date:_____

This choice is presented to the teenager at what we call the "structured intervention." The time for contracts is over. The teenager must go into treatment. By breaking the Bottom-Line Contract, the teenager has shown that he or she is addicted to alcohol/drugs and no longer capable of choosing to use or not. Being responsible to the teenager necessitates removing him or her from the home and the school and into the protective environment of a treatment center.

The structured intervention is a group process. It should never be attempted by the parents alone, the school alone, the court alone, or any agency acting independently. It is best accomplished by a network — a united front — of significant people who have been identified and educated about the disease of chemical dependence. This identification and education should have occurred in the disengagement stage.

It is important that the group include at least one connector — the "cookie person." Without the presence of someone the teenager trusts, someone who accepts the teenager without reservation, the confrontation may come across as an attack.

We recommend that you practice the Structured Intervention before actually doing it with your teenager. Don't go in unprepared! We also recommend — and recommend very highly — that you let your professional caregiver direct both the practice session and the real sessions. You will experience support and realize that you are not alone. You will learn to anticipate your feelings and your teenager's reactions. And you will be clear on the choices you are giving your teenager.

Step Three: Learning Confrontation Skills

There are three skills you will need to effectively control the environment with choices, consequences, and contracts: *monitoring skills, giving feedback* to your teenager, and *consequating.*

1. Monitoring Skills

When you put your teenager on a contract, you must be willing to monitor and record his or her behaviors.

One way to approach this (illustrated in the Sample Contracts) is by making an "X" under the day when the behavior or task is scheduled to be done. Then all you have to do is circle the "X" when your teenager does it.

For example, Julie, your daughter, has signed a Turf Contract. She has agreed to come home by 10:00 on week nights and 12:30 on weekend nights and to attend school every day. Here is what those portions of her contract look like after a week:

BEHAVIOR/TASK	POSSIBLE POINTS	S	M	T	W	TH	F	S	TOTAL
Keeping curfews 10:00 week night 12:30 week end	10	Ⓧ	Ⓧ	Ⓧ	Ⓧ	X			/50
							Ⓧ	Ⓧ	/20
School attendance (all classes)	10	Ⓧ	Ⓧ	Ⓧ	Ⓧ	X			/50

Add up the circled X's and write the accumulated points under "Total."

BEHAVIOR/TASK	POSSIBLE POINTS	S	M	T	W	TH	F	S	TOTAL
Keeping curfews 10:00 week night 12:30 week end	10	Ⓧ	Ⓧ	Ⓧ	Ⓧ	X			40/50
							Ⓧ	Ⓧ	20/20
School attendance (all classes)	10	Ⓧ	Ⓧ	Ⓧ	Ⓧ	X			40/50

Julie has earned 100 points out of a possible 120.

Monitoring behaviors in this way keeps you from enabling. You don't have to nag or threaten; all you have to do is circle and add. You are not responsible for the behaviors — your teenager is.

It also keeps you from "snoopervision." You don't have to be a sneak or a private detective. Just be a supervisor of your environment.

It also lets both you and your teenager keep your self-respect because everything is up front. You both know what's happening on a daily basis.

Finally, it gives you the data necessary for any further confrontation you may need to do.

Monitoring is easy, once you form the habit. *Be sure to do it daily.* Record the behaviors as they are performed. **Don't rely on your memory**; the teenager (and you) must be able to trust what's on the contract as true and reliable information.

2. Giving Feedback

When you put your teenager on a contract, you must be willing to give him or her feedback on what you learn from monitoring and recording his or her behaviors.

At the end of each week, tell your teenager how many points he or she earned. Based on these points, you can then tell the teenager whether he or she kept the contract and earned the privileges described in it. The contract makes this a simple matter of adding up the points and comparing the total to the minimums required. It's a black-and-white, thoroughly objective process: "Bill, you made 270 out of 300 points this week. You needed 285 points to use the car."

Describe the behaviors you recorded: "You came in late on Thursday night, you were verbally abusive to your father, and you skipped school on Friday. That cost you 30 points."

When doing a structured intervention, it will be important to connect the teenager's behaviors to the symptoms of chemical dependence. This will help the teenager to see that he or she has become harmfully dependent on alcohol/drugs. Practice making these connections with your professional caregiver. You might say something like this:

"Bill, you missed school on Friday because you had a hangover. You also lost your job because of alcohol on your breath. You hit your mother and your brother on two occasions during the day after you got out of bed, and you say that you don't even remember doing it. These are all signs of chemical dependence."

Don't limit your feedback to your teenager's behaviors. Be prepared to talk about *how you feel* about those behaviors. Practice this with your professional caregiver, your spouse, or a friend, using these three statements as starting points:

— "When you. . . ." (Describe the behavior)
— "I feel. . ." (Identify your feelings)
— "Because you. . ." (Give the effects of the behavior)

For example:

• "When you come home drunk, I feel scared because you could become an alcoholic."
• "When you drink and drive, I feel anxious and afraid because you could kill someone else or yourself, and I care."
• "When you skip school, I feel scared and worried because you may never graduate."

Giving feedback will keep you from being a Provoker. It will also allow you to express your caring feelings without giving way to anger.

3. Consequating

"Consequating" is an all-purpose word we use to describe

what you should do when a teenager doesn't meet the terms of a contract. It involves letting natural consequences happen and enforcing logical consequences.

Consequating means letting your teenager sit on his or her own blisters. It means taking a stand, establishing rules in your home (especially the "No Use" rule), and sticking to them. It means backing up the school's regulations (especially those having to do with alcohol/drug use). It means supporting the laws in your community (especially those regarding chemical use). It means being consistent: a consequence is a consequence, there are no two ways about it, and there are no second chances.

Consequating will keep you from becoming permissive. It will keep you from being manipulated and allow you to regain control of your environment. It will also keep you from giving up during what can be a difficult, demanding, and draining process. Consequating gives you strength, and it gives your teenager a sense of security — of knowing beyond a doubt what will happen next.

True, your teenager may not like you during this process. Your teenager may even hate you for a while. Don't be surprised — and don't back down. By consequating with consistency, you will be giving your teenager what he or she needs most: a parent who can be counted on, who means what he or she says, who can be trusted, and who clearly cares.

Eight Tips to Help You Confront

Confrontation isn't easy. It may be the hardest thing you ever do, especially if you have to go all the way to a structured intervention. But it may also be the most important thing you ever do. You're playing for high stakes: your child's life.

1. Never humiliate your teenager. Always confront with respect. Offer choices; this lets your teenager save face.

2. Let your teenager experience his or her own pain. Don't rob your teenager of the right to struggle through it. Be there and be supportive, but don't try to ease the pain or take it on yourself.

3. NEVER confront your teenager while he or she is under the influence of alcohol/drugs. He or she may be in a blackout. Wait until your teenager is sober or (even better) suffering from a hangover.

4. Don't be permissive. Set up a "No Use" rule, then stick to it. Take a stand! Monitor, give feedback, and consequate as needed.

5. Don't "snoopervise." Respect your teenager's privacy. Monitor behaviors, but don't go on spy missions through your teenager's room or belongings unless his or her behaviors become self-destructive. Then do whatever is necessary to help.

6. Don't make threats you can't enforce. Instead, establish consequences that you're willing and able to enforce. Keep them logical and natural. Get your teenager involved in setting rules for his or her behavior at home.

7. Try not to see your teenager as a "monster" or a "bum" — even though it may be tempting at times. Instead, give encouragement and lots of love.

8. Don't try to go it alone. Seek information and support from outside resources. Find out what's available in your community, then make use of it. Among adolescents, chemical dependence is a system disease; it takes a system to crack a system.

13

The Professional's Role in Confrontation

What you do after the first group meeting will depend on what level of usage the teenager is at. For teenagers at levels 1, 2, or 3, your role may consist of helping the parents and schools to draw up the contracts and decide on the choices and consequences. You may also serve as a source of information, advice, and encouragement for parents, teachers, and others involved in the intervention.

Where you will be needed most urgently is in confrontations with Level 4 teenagers who have broken the Bottom-Line Contract. The structured intervention is the most difficult and demanding of all confrontations, and it is also the one that is most similar to the intervention used with adult chemical dependents.

Your first responsibility will be to guide the key people involved in the intervention through a rehearsal of the structured intervention. We recommend the following steps.

1. Choose a group leader.

This person will direct the structured intervention and speak for the group. Someone *other than the teenager's parent* should be chosen. There are usually too many conflicting emotions between the parent and the chemical dependent. Also, it's important to avoid having the teenager feel as though intervention is being done solely at the urging of the parent. They teenager should understand clearly that *many concerned persons* are involved.

While you, as the professional, can lead the session, it's more effective if someone else (such as a teacher, counselor, or coach) whom the teenager already knows, respects, and finds very credible assumes that role. At the structured intervention, you can introduce yourself to the teenager and say that these people have gathered out of concern for him or her and one another, and that they'd like to share what those concerns are. The leader can then take over with occasional assistance from you when necessary.

2. Go over the written lists prepared by the group members.

Unlike intervention with adults, structured intervention with teenagers focuses mainly on the Bottom-Line Contract. The teenager agreed in advance to the consequences of breaking that contract. He or she knows what those consequences involve. During the structured intervention, you and the group will restate those consequences, give the student feedback on his or her behavior, and let the teenager know how and when the consequences are to be enforced.

Basically, the structured intervention involves telling the teenager, "Your points add up to less than the 90% required for you to keep living at home and going to school. The consequence is going into treatment."

The teenager impaired by delusion may not be able to understand or accept this. That is why the structured intervention also involves having each person in the group present reality to the teenager in a receivable way. This is done by describing at least one alcohol/drug-related behavior and how it has affected the person.

During the disengagement stage, you asked each group

member to gather data about the teenager's alcohol/drug use. Now devote part of the practice session to going over that data and helping each person to choose at least one concern to present during the structured intervention.

Here are some examples of what group members might tell the teenager:

- "When you come high and hit your mother like you did yesterday, I really worry about what's happening to you. It's not like you to do that."
- "When you didn't go to school last week because you were too hungover every morning, I got scared. I care about what you are going to do with your life."
- "Last Saturday night when you were drunk and talked about killing yourself, I felt afraid that you just might do it."
- "When you drink and drive like you did last week, I am afraid that you might kill somebody else or even yourself."
- "When you were drunk and drove across the school lawn last week, I got embarrassed because people talked about you and us."
- "When you came home high last night and shouted and hollered, I felt sad because you seem to be so unhappy with your life."

3. Decide the order in which group members will speak.

In general, family members should speak after teachers, counselors, coaches, probation officers, employers, friends, and others outside the immediate family have had their say. These people help break down the teenager's resistance to listening to the data. Then, when the family members do speak (and present the most powerful and convincing data), the teenager is more prepared to hear it.

4. Decide on a seating arrangement.

Avoid having the teenager sit near the door; this makes it too easy for him or her to leave the room impulsively. Putting others in front of the door presents a psychological barrier.

Avoid seating the parents close to the teenager; this enables him or her to focus anger and fear on them and disregard the group.

Have the leader or "cookie person" sit next to the teenager. The leader is objective; the "cookie person" is accepting. Either can help the teenager become more receptive to the idea of treatment.

5. Decide where the structured intervention will take place.

It should *not* take place in the teenager's home. Acceptable alternatives include your office, the school counselor's office, or other reasonably neutral ground. You may want to schedule it for the same classroom the teenager goes to for second-phase intervention group sessions.

6. Choose a person to act as the teenager during the rehearsal.

Have him or her respond as the teenager is likely to. Meanwhile, watch for anger, resentment, opinions, and judgments among group members. Use this time to help them work through their feelings.

Remind the group members that they will have to stay on task, especially when the teenager is desperately trying to push any and all buttons.

7. Conduct the rehearsal.

After doing steps 1 through 6, have the group take a break, stretch, even leave the room — and come back prepared to do and say the things you have planned for the structured intervention. This means sitting according to the seating arrangement and having their statements prepared. The person playing the teenager should enter the room after everyone else has arrived and taken their seats.

- Start by summarizing why everyone is at the meeting. Direct your comments toward the "teenager." You might say something like this:

> "Jennifer, we're all here because we care about you and are concerned about what you're doing to yourself and others. We all know that you haven't been able to follow the terms of your Bottom-Line Contract. By breaking that contract, you've let us know that you can't control your chemical use. That tells us you need help — our help. We're here to share our concern about your behavior and to tell you about the consequences of breaking the contract."

- Set the ground rules. For example:

> "This is going to be difficult for you and for all of us. I want you to agree to let each one of us share our concern and promise to listen. I know it's not going to be easy, but I want you to agree not to respond until everyone else has spoken first. Just listen. Later you'll have the chance to respond."

This agreement is critical to structured intervention. Whenever the teenager tries to respond to or interrupt someone who is sharing a concern, calmly restate it.

- Have the group members present the concerns you practiced earlier. Follow the speaking order you decided on earlier.

- Review the choices and consequences outlined in the Bottom-Line Contract. For example:

  "Jennifer, when you signed this contract, you agreed to follow its terms. Since you haven't been able to do this, the consequence is going into treatment. You have a choice. You can go to either of these two in-patient treatment centers: _____ or _____. Which will it be?"

NOTE: It's vital to choose the two treatment centers *before* the structured intervention takes place, and to ensure that both are ready to receive the teenager. It's also vital that you, the professional, inform the staff of the treatment center that is chosen about the results of the structured intervention. They need to know what to expect before the teenager arrives.

- Close by summarizing the concerns of the group.

When the time comes to do the actual structured intervention, everyone should be reasonably ready for it. Your primary role will involve making sure that the group members do what they've prepared themselves to do — in other words, helping them to stay on track.

On the day of the structured intervention, group members should arrive at least an hour ahead of time. This gives you a chance to make sure that the arrangements with the treatment centers have been taken care of, and that everyone knows his or her part in the process.

At the end of the session, the teenager may not accept treatment as the only option. Here's where things can degenerate quickly into a shouting match or a contest of wills. A good way to avoid this is by following this simple script:

Leader: "You have a choice. You can either go into in-patient treatment at _____ , or at _____ ."

Teenager: "What if I don't choose either?"

Leader: "Then you have just made a choice to be turned over to the court. They will send you to the treatment center they choose."
Teenager: "What kind of choice is that?"
Leader: "It's your choice."

The teenager should go into treatment as soon as possible — even as early as immediately after the structured intervention. The parents might have a suitcase packed and waiting in the car.

Again, it's vital to *plan in advance* for a teenager's admission to the treatment centers. Make sure that nothing happens to prevent the earliest possible admission. Courtesy demands that the treatment center not chosen be notified immediately.

The sooner the teenager starts treatment, the sooner the harmful dependence on alcohol/drugs can be arrested.

THE INTERVENTION PROCESS: SUMMARY

Levels of Usage	Activity	Control	Consequences with Choices
Learns Mood Swing USE	Normal activities	"No Use" rule	Suspension (home, school, or group)
Seeks Mood Swing MISUSE	1st phase information group	Simple Contract	Evaluation (out-patient or in-patient)
Harmfully Involved ABUSE	2nd phase intervention group	Turf Contract	Treatment (out-patient or in-patient)
Harmfully Dependent ADDICTION	Counseling (out-patient)	Bottom-Line Contract	In-patient treatment

14

Reintegration: Following Up Intervention

The third stage of successful intervention focuses on issues of sobriety. Your teenager has stopped using alcohol/drugs — either because he or she has been able to follow the terms of the "No Use" rule or one of the contracts, or because he or she has gone through treatment. Now it's time to support the reality of living without chemicals.

During reintegration, the teenager learns to work through the painful feelings of being an adolescent. With your help and the support of other caring persons, he or she enters the process of being "habilitated" — learning to handle the tasks of adolescence. During reintegration, you and all other members of your family start to reclaim the power you lost or gave away while your teenager was using alcohol/drugs.

The theme for this stage is Let Go. You will continue doing what you began during disengagement — letting go of trying to control your teenager's behaviors, feelings, and decisions. *You will also let go of your expectations for your teenager.* This is hard enough to do with a teenager who has never been in trouble with alcohol/drugs. For the teenager coming out of treatment, it is even more difficult.

After going through disengagement and confrontation, it's tempting to think that you're home free. It seems reasonable to expect your teenager to shed all of the objectionable and rebellious behaviors he or she exhibited while using. The using has stopped, and so should the behaviors — or so you believe. Wrong! Objectionable and rebellious behaviors are *normal* for adolescence. Even those that were directly related to the using may be hard to shake off or change, and you can bet that they will be replaced by some others you may not like or understand. *Don't expect your teenager to be perfect.*

It also seems reasonable to expect your teenager to stay straight. You spent a lot of time and energy getting him or her into treatment; he or she spent a lot of time and energy in treatment. The truth is, treatment doesn't always solve the problem the first time around.

Some teenagers have to go back once, twice, and even more before they can really start recovering. They will certainly need to be involved in a structured aftercare or support group for at least one to two years. Attendance at A.A., N.A., or C.A. is also strongly recommended.

Donna was 17 years old when she tried to commit suicide in jail. She was placed on a psychiatric unit for care and evaluation, after which she was transferred to a chemical dependence treatment center.

She went through the motions. Somehow she was able to sneak drugs into the treatment center, and she used them. She lied, and she manipulated the staff and the other patients. When writing the history of her drug usage and how it had affected her, she simply copied the history she found recorded in her roommate's journal and changed the details.

When she arrived back home, her parents told her that if she drank or used other drugs again, she would go back to treatment. If she wanted to remain at home, she would have to abide by the terms of the Bottom-Line Contract. She lasted three days and got drunk the third night. The next day, she found herself in treatment again.

This time it was different. Donna chose to stay straight. She listened to the lectures. She started sharing her feelings with her counselor and getting honest with the other members of her group. But she still couldn't believe that she, a 17-year-old girl, could be chemically dependent.

Upon her discharge from treatment, she was placed in a group home, where she stayed sober for three weeks. Then she went out and got drunk. Afterward she attended an open A.A. meeting with her friends. It was there that the reality of her chemical dependence finally hit her. Feeling hungover and miserable, she heard one of the speakers laugh at himself. And she thought, "That's what I want to be able to do."

Donna has been sober ever since. In fact, she recently celebrated her tenth anniversary of sobriety. But consider all the places she'd been before she walked through the door of the A.A. meeting: jail, a psychiatric unit, treatment (twice), and a group home.

You just can't control when and where a teenager will accept reality and see the light. All you can do is keep controlling yourself and your environment.

You may be discouraged if your teenager starts drinking or using again after returning home from treatment. *Don't take it personally*. Remember that intervention is a process. Keep the Bottom-Line Contract in effect for the first two weeks. Keep enforcing the "No Use" rule. Let your teenager know that the consequences of breaking the contract will mean treatment again — and again, and again, for as long and as often as it takes.*

There are three steps to reintegration: *supporting yourself in sobriety, supporting your teenager in sobriety,* and *developing a creative home environment.*

---

* For more help in dealing with your expectations, read *Recovery of Chemically Dependent Families*, revised edition (Minneapolis: Johnson Institute, 1987).

Step One: Supporting Yourself in Sobriety

Your work on your own behalf has just begun. Remember that chemical dependence is a family disease. You have been affected, too.*

- Continue with the activities you began during disengagement — making time for your needs, relaxing, taking "minute vacations." Keep growing in self-love!
- Continue going to Families Anonymous or Al-Anon or whatever self-help group you joined during the disengagement stage. The Twelve Steps work, but they do take time. Eventually they become a way of life.
- See a counselor if you need more help with unresolved issues. You may find that treatment will benefit you as well as your teenager.
- Stay in the network of concerned persons you formed to help your teenager. Keep communicating with the school, the courts, and treatment centers. Don't assume that your other children will never get in trouble with alcohol/drugs just because they've seen what it can do to their sibling. Be prepared!

Step Two: Supporting Your Teenager in Sobriety

What can you realistically expect from a teenager who has just come out of treatment?

At first, you can expect your teenager to be excited about having made new friends, having shared his or her feelings, having discovered a program that has helped others to stay straight, and having reconnected with you and other members of your family.

---

* To understand how chemical dependence affects families, read *Chemical Dependence and Recovery: A Family Affair*, revised edition (Minneapolis: Johnson Institute, 1987).

You can also expect this excitement to cool down, and soon.

You can expect your teenager to "12th step" all over the place — to try to get his or her friends to stop using and go to treatment if necessary (and even if not necessary). There is a tendency to want to save everybody and shout "the good news of sobriety" from the rooftops.

You can also expect this enthusiasm to diminish somewhat.

Above all, you can expect your teenager to be struggling with adolescence. Remember that the delusion caused by chemical dependence effectively prevents a teenager from achieving the four basic goals of adolescence: to achieve independence, to develop integrity, to experience intimacy, and to develop one's individuality. It also makes it impossible for the teenager to meet the four basic self-esteem needs: to be somebody, to go beyond, to belong, and to be oneself.

Alcohol/drug dependence results in impairment at all levels: physical, emotional, mental, and spiritual. Emotional growth is arrested. Often a teenager just out of treatment feels like a little child who must face the cold, hard world alone. There is (understandably) a lot of fear and trembling.

For the recovering teenager, each task of adolescence is complicated by the added task of staying sober.

- **Achieving independence from one's family might involve:**
    - starting to learn simple living skills like cooking, budgeting, washing clothes, cleaning the house, and buying groceries
    - changing schools because of the lack of support from teachers and other students (or to avoid old alcohol/drug using friends)
    - looking for work without having acquired any job skills, training, or discipline for keeping timetables

- **Developing integrity might involve:**
  - attending self-help groups (A.A., N.A., C.A.) two or three times a week (even daily) and structured aftercare or support groups weekly
  - finding a church that teaches about a forgiving and personal God
  - learning what to do with leisure time that used to be spent drunk or high (exercise, reading, music, art, crafts)

- **Experiencing intimacy might involve:**
  - changing old using friends for new straight ones (usually people met in the program)
  - establishing trust with one's parents, starting from scratch (at this point there is no trust)
  - accepting one's sexuality with all of its hangups, and learning the difference between affection and seduction

- **Developing one's individuality might involve:**
  - dealing with feelings, especially anger, in assertive and constructive ways
  - changing from the drinking/drug culture lifestyle to a chemical-free lifestyle
  - facing unresolved grief issues due to past losses and abuses

It can help tremendously if a teenager has a sponsor — a "cookie person" who can also serve as a model for sobriety. Many professional caregivers believe that a sponsor is crucial to a successful first year of recovery.

These are all issues of sobriety when faced by a recovering teenager. Young people need to be allowed to work through them by themselves. Be there for your teenager; walk with him or her; offer support — but let your teenager do the work.

Step Three: Developing a Creative Home Environment

A chemically dependent teenager who emerges from treatment straight and sober is a changed person. Welcome him or her into a creative home environment. By "creative," we mean one in which people *encourage* one another, *listen* to one another, and know how to *problem-solve.*

• Giving Encouragement

Teenagers need praise and encouragement — especially if chemical dependence has robbed them of their self-esteem for months or years.

Be positive with your teenager. Be supportive. Smile!

Praise recognizes the thing accomplished: "Good job!" It is conditional and specific: "I like the way you did the dishes." "I respect the way you've been concentrating on your homework." "I appreciate your mowing the lawn." Encouragement recognizes the effort put into the thing accomplished: "Tell me how you did that!" It is unconditional and less specific: "You are special." "I like you a lot."

Giving encouragement taps the teenager's inner courage to grow from within, where the real power is (clearness, closeness, curiosity, creativity). It helps the teenager learn to do internal evaluations ("I am good at studying; I am a caring person.") It builds self-esteem and feelings of worth ("I am somebody; I do belong; I am unique.")

Remember that the recovering teenager must meet his or her self-esteem needs *without chemicals* — a new and intimidating task. He or she needs support from you, other family members, teachers, friends, and whoever else can offer it.

• Listening

Start tuning in to what your teenager is trying to say. Stay in the "here and now" and also pay attention to what the teenager is *not* saying. This takes time, concentration, and the willingness to admit that you don't always have the answers. ("It sounds to me like you're having trouble making new friends. That can be scary and hard to do, and I can't tell you how to do it. None of us are real experts at it!" Or: "You look sad today. Is it because your old friends are still using?")

Is your teenager feeling pleasure, or pain? Work with him or her to find out. Rephrase the words he or she uses and bounce back the feeling you think he or she is experiencing. ("You seem discouraged about your progress in school this first six weeks." Or: "You're really excited today. Tell me what happened in school!")

When you really listen to your children, you are telling them they are worthwhile because you are spending time with them. You are telling them they are special because you are paying attention to them. You are letting them know you care.

• Problem-Solving

This is a learned skill that takes practice. It's the skill you will use as you continue to make rules and set up contracts. It's a skill that all of your children will carry with them for life — if you teach them. And it's essential for the teenager in recovery.

Let's say your son is going to a party where there will be drinking. You both know it, and you're concerned. He's been attending his group meetings regularly. Your concern is not that *he* will drink, but that he'll be in a car with others who will. What can you do?

One easy-to-use and easy-to-remember formula for problem-solving is **DIG EDDE**. It goes like this:

Determine a time and place to meet.

You: "Son, I would like to meet with you after dinner in the family room. We need to talk about the party tonight."

Identify the problem.

You: "I understand that there's going to be beer at the party. I think we may have a problem here. How are you going to get home? I'm concerned that you might end up in a car where the driver has been drinking."

Generate alternatives.

Listen as your teenager suggests some possibilities. Don't dismiss or discount any of them; write each one down in turn.

You: "If you learn that a driver has been drinking, what can you do besides get in the car?"
Your son: "Well, I could walk. I could call a taxi. I could call you to pick me up. I could see if anyone with a driver's license doesn't drink and will drive me home. I could stay at home and not go."

Evaluate each alternative.

Be honest about your feelings, if applicable.

You: "It's too far to walk. If you call a taxi, I'll pay half the fare. I'm willing to pick you up. I feel comfortable with your finding a driver who hasn't been drinking. And I like the idea of your staying home best of all."

Decide on a plan.

Be as specific as possible.

Your son: "I will see if someone who isn't drinking will drive me home. If I can't find anyone, I'll call a taxi."

Do it!

You: "Okay, that sounds reasonable to me."

Evaluate the outcome at a predetermined time.

You: "We'll meet tonight when you get home. I plan to be up anyway."

What's important in problem-solving isn't the end result, but the process of getting there. Simply by taking the time to identify a problem, generate alternatives and solutions, and evaluate each one according to its merits, you'll be giving your teenager skills that will last forever.

You can use your encouraging, listening, and problem-solving skills all at the same time within the context of a family meeting. It's a good idea to hold family meetings when planning activities and addressing concerns. Meet on a weekly basis — for example, on Sunday afternoon or evening. Choose a time when everyone in the family can be there, then ask them to commit to it.

Decisions made at family meetings are made by consensus, not by a dictator (like a parent) or even by a majority vote. Consensus demands that you listen to one another. Everyone's concerns are given equal weight and consideration, regardless of how important or trivial they may seem to you, and regardless of the family member's age. Consensus also demands that you accept and support a decision even if you don't particularly like it.

If consensus can't be reached, table any decision until the next meeting. This will give each family member time to think things through. By waiting until you are able to reach consensus, you will teach your children the value of cooperation.

Choose a chairperson to run the meeting. Have a different member of the family do it each week. This way, everyone becomes important.

Here's a suggested format for family meetings:

1. **Start with positives.** Have each family member say something positive about every other family member, or something he or she feels good about at the moment. Use encouragement liberally, and be specific. ("Steve, I really appreciated your willingness to help me clean the garage on Saturday, especially because I know you had other plans.")

2. **Review the coming week's activities.** Use a calendar to schedule school activities, sports, self-help groups, dates, and work. Listen.

3. **Problem-solve any identified concerns or troubles.** Use DIG EDDE. Set up rules and consequences; be sure to solicit input on these from the other family members. By asking for everyone's opinion and listening carefully as it's delivered, you will teach your children the importance of respect.

4. **Plan at least one fun activity** — a movie, a trip to the zoo or a museum, a picnic at the park, a baseball game — for the whole family. Do this at every meeting. If your plans include a vacation sometime in the future, be sure to also arrange for something during the coming week.

5. **End on a positive note** (a special treat or game).

Above all, be sure you begin to practice the open, honest, and accepted act of sharing feelings with one another — both negative and positive. Avoid the "don't talk, don't trust, don't feel" rules that often govern families with chemically dependent parents or children. These rules stifle love and force family members apart.

Family meetings, if held regularly, help to produce creative environments. They also give support to recovering teenagers who are struggling to meet and address their sobriety issues.

Finally, they challenge all family members to discover and explore their own inner qualities. Children and adults who are encouraged and praised, listened to, respected, and valued for themselves are free to find out what it means to be oneself. They are free to become whoever they are and develop fully as human beings.

*   *   *

As you struggle with your teenager — to determine whether he or she is using alcohol/drugs, to find out the level of usage, to break through the layers of the delusional system, to confront and confront until your teenager gets the message and chooses to change — please be assured of our deep concern, our prayers, and our belief that *you can do it*. Thousands of parents already have; thousands of teenagers today are recovering because their parents cared enough to act, and professionals cared enough to help.

Part III

RESOURCES

The following are some of the books, booklets, and videos available from Hazelden. Please call our toll free number, 1-800-328-9000 for ordering information or to ask for a free catalog.

Books

Bell, Peter. Growing Up Black and Proud: A Curriculum for African American Youth. Order #P226(Facilitator's Guide) and #P227 (Teen Guide).

Cohen, Peter, M.D. *Helping Your Chemically Dependent Teenager Recover.* Order #P179.

Fleming, Martin. *Conducting Support Group Activities for Students Affected by Chemical Dependence.* Order #P020.

_____. *How To Stay Clean and Sober: A Relapse Prevention Guide for Teenagers.* Order #P167.

_____. *101 Support Group Activities for Teenagers Affected by Someone Else's Alcohol/Drug Use.* Order #P212.

_____. *101 Support Group Activities for Teenagers At Risk for Chemical Dependence or Related Problems.* Order #P214.

_____. *101 Support Group Activities for Teenagers Recovering from Chemical Dependence.* Order #P213.

_____. *Take Charge of Your Life: What To Do When Someone in Your Family Has a Drinking or Other Drug Problem—A Guide for Teenagers.* Order #P263.

Freeman, Shelley MacKay. *From Peer Pressure to Peer Support: Alcohol and Other Drug Prevention Through Group Process (A Curriculum for Grades 7-8)*. Order #P147-7-8.

_____. *From Peer Pressure to Peer Support: Alcohol and Other Drug Prevention Through Group Process (A Curriculum for Grades 9-10)*. Order #P147-9-10.

_____. *From Peer Pressure to Peer Support: Alcohol and Other Drug Prevention Through Group Process (A Curriculum for Grades 11-12)*. Order #P147-11-12.

Johnson Institute. *Training Families to Do a Successful Intervention*. Order #P552.

Johnson, Vernon E. *Everything You Need to Know About Chemical Dependence: Vernon Johnson's Complete Guide for Families*. Order #P011.

_____. *Intervention: How To Help Someone Who Doesn't Want Help—A Step-By-Step Guide for Families and Friends of Chemically Dependent Persons*. Order #P140.

Leite, Evelyn, and Pamela Espeland. *Different Like Me: A Book for Teens Who Worry About Their Parents' Use of Alcohol/Drugs*. Order #P097.

Remboldt, Carole. *Good Intentions, Bad Results: Am I An Enabler?* Order #P309.

_____. *How Chemical Use Becomes Chemical Dependence*. Order #P310.

Sassatelli, Jean. *Breaking Away: Saying Goodbye to Alcohol/Drugs—A Guide to Help Teenagers Stop Using Chemicals*. Order #P058.

Schmidt, Teresa, and Thelma Spencer. *Tanya Talks About Chemical Dependence in the Family (Grades 6-8)*. Order #P164.

Wilmes, David J. *Alcohol is a Drug, Too: What Happens to Kids When We're Afraid To Say No*. Order #P231.

_____. *Parenting for Prevention—A Parent Education Curriculum: Raising a Child To Say No to Alcohol and Other Drugs.* Order #P072TK

_____. *Parenting for Prevention: How To Raise a Child To Say No to Alcohol/Drugs.* Order #P071.

Zarek, David, and James Sipe. *Can I Handle Alcohol/Drugs? A Self-Assessment Guide for Youth.* Order #P095.

Booklets

Alcoholism: A Treatable Disease. Order #P112.

Anger: How To Handle It During Recovery. Order #P017.

Avoiding Power Plays with Kids. Order #P007-10.

Chemical Dependence and Rcovery: A Family Affair. Order #P104.

Chemical Dependence: Yes, You Can Do Something. Order #P099.

Detachment: The Art of Letting Go While Living with an Alcoholic. Order #P105.

Detachment vs. Intervention: Is There a Conflict?. Order #P033.

Enabling in the School Setting. Order #P082.

Facts About Kids' Use of Alcohol and Other Drugs. Order #P007-11

Family Enablers, The. Order #P114.

Helping Kids Be Responsible for Themselves. Order #P007-9.

Helping Kids Communicate. Order #P007-4.

Helping Kids Feel Good About Themselves. P007-8.

Helping Kids Learn Refusal Skills. Order #P007-5.

Helping Kids Make Decisions. Order #P007-7.

Helping Kids Understand Their Feelings. Order #P007-3.

Helping Teens From Alcoholic Families. Order #P233.

How Chemical Dependence Differs for Adults and Teenagers. Order #P007-12.

How It Feels To Be Chemically Dependent. Order #P098.

How To Control Your Anger Before It Controls You. Order #P277.

Is Your Child Involved with Alcohol and Other Drugs? Order #P007-6.

Job Description for Kids, A. Order #P007-2.

Job Description for Parents, A. Order #P007-1.

Recovery of Chemically Dependent Families. Order #P117.

When Your Child Is Chemically Dependent. Order #P182.

Why Haven't I Been Able To Help? Order #P119.

Videos

Anger: Handle It Before It Handles You. Color,15 min. Order #V450.

Another Chance To Change. Color, 30 min. Order #V422.

Back to Reality. Color, 33 min. Order #V408.

Choices & Consequences: Intervention with Youth in Trouble with Alcohol/Drugs. Color, 33 min. Order #V400.

Conflict: Think About It, Talk About It, Try To Work It Out. Color, 15 min. Order #V451.

Different Like Me. Color, 30 min. Order #V412.

Enabling: Masking Reality. Color, 22 min. Order #V409.

Good Intentions, Bad Results. Color, 30 min. Order #V440.

Intervention: Facing Reality. Color, 30 min. Order #V410.

Kids At Risk: A Four-Part Video Series for Middle School Children:
  Covering up for Kevin. Color, 17 min. Order #V427.
  Blaming Kitty. Color, 18 min. Order #V428.
  An Attitude Adjustment for Ramie. Color, 15 min. Order #V429.
  Double Bind. Color, 15 min. Order #V430.

Mirror of a Child, The. Color, 30 min. Order #V411.

Where's Shelley? Color, 13 min. Order #V405.

For more information, or to order any of these publications or videos, call or write:

Hazelden Information and Educational Services

Center City, MN 55012-0176

1-800-328-9000 (Toll free U.S., Canada, and the Virgin Islands)

1-651-213-4000 (Outside the U.S. and Canada)

1-651-213-4590 (24-hour Fax)

www.hazelden.org

When ordering, be sure to request a copy of our catalog.

The Twelve Steps

1. We admitted we were powerless over alcohol — that our lives had become unmanageable.

2. Came to believe that a Power greater than ourselves could restore us to sanity.

3. Made a decision to turn our will and our lives over to the care of God as *we understood Him.*

4. Made a searching and fearless moral inventory of ourselves.

5. Admitted to God, to ourselves, and to another human being the exact nature of our wrongs.

6. Were entirely ready to have God remove all these defects of character.

7. Humbly asked Him to remove our shortcomings.

8. Made a list of all persons we had harmed, and became willing to make amends to them all.

9. Made direct amends to such people wherever possible, except when to do so would injure them or others.

10. Continued to take personal inventory and when we were wrong promptly admitted it.

11. Sought through prayer and meditation to improve our conscious contact with God *as we understood Him*, praying only for knowledge of His will for us and the power to carry that out.

12. Having had a spiritual awakening as the result of these steps, we tried to carry this message to alcoholics, and to practice these principles in all our affairs.

From Alcoholics Anonymous, Third Edition *(New York: Alcoholics Anonymous World Services, Inc., 1976), p. 59. Reprinted with permission of Alcoholics Anonymous World Services, Inc.*

Resources

National Organizations

The following groups and organizations can provide additional information on preventing alcohol and other drug use by children and adolescents.

A.A.
Alcoholics Anonymous
General Service Office
P.O. Box 459
Grand Central Station
New York, NY 10163
(212) 686-1100

Addiction Research Foundation
33 Russell Street
Toronto, Ontario
M5S 2S1, Canada
(416) 595-6056

Al-Anon Family Group
  Headquarters
1372 Broadway
New York, NY 10018-0862
(212) 302-7240

Alateen
1372 Broadway
New York, NY 10018-0862
(212) 302-7240

American Council for Drug
  Education
204 Monroe Street
Rockville, MD 20850
(301) 294-0600

COAF
Children of Alcoholics
  Foundation, Inc.
555 Madison Avenue, 20th Floor
New York, NY 10022
(212) 754-0656

Families Anonymous
World Service Office
P.O. Box 528
Van Nuys, CA 91408
(818) 989-7841

Hazelden
15251 Pleasant Valley Road
P.O. Box 176
Center City, MN 55012-0176
1-800-328-9000

IBCA
Institute on Black Chemical Abuse
2614 Nicollet Avenue South
Minneapolis, MN 55408
(612) 871-7878

Johnson Institute
7205 Ohms Lane
Minneapolis, MN 55439
1-800-231-5165

Just Say No International
2101 Webster Street, Suite 1300
Oakland, CA 94612
(510) 451-6666
1-800-258-2766

National Association for Children
  of Alcoholics, Inc.
(NACOA)
11426 Rockville Pike
Suite 100
Rockville, MD 20852
(301) 468-0985

Narcotics Anonymous (NA)
World Services Office, Inc.
P.O. Box 9999
Van Nuys, CA 91409
(818) 733-9999
(818) 700-0700

National Coalition for the
  Prevention of Drug and Alcohol
  Abuse
537 Jones Road
Granville, OH 43023
(614) 587-2800

National Council of Alcoholism
and Drug Dependence
(NCADD)
12 West 21st Street
New York, NY 10010
(212) 206-6770

National Federation of Parents
  for Drug-Free Youth
8730 Georgia Avenue, Suite 200
Silver Spring, MD 20910
(301) 585-5437

National Council on Alcoholism
(NCA)
12 West 21st Street, 7th Floor
New York, NY 10010
1-800-NCA-CALL

National Clearing house for
  Alcohol/Drug Information
(NCADI)
11426 Rockville Pike
Rockville, MD 28052
(301) 468-2600

National Institute on Alcohol
  Abuse and Alcoholism
(NIAAA)
6000 Executive Blvd.
Bethesda, MD 20892-7003
(301) 443-3885

National Institute of Drug Abuse
(NIDA)
Room 10-05, Parklawn Building
5600 Fishers Lane
Rockville, MD 20857
(301) 443-6480

National Parents Resource
 Institute on Drug Education
(PRIDE)
10 Park Place South, Suite 540
Atlanta, GA 30303
(404) 577-4500

NCA
National Council on Alcoholism
 and Drug Dependence Hopeline
12 West 21st Street, 7th Floor
New York, NY 10010
1-800-NCA-CALL

Students Against Drunk Driving
(SADD)
P.O. Box 800
277 Main Street
Marlboro, MA 01752
1-800-521-SADD

SAMPLE SCHOOL CHECKLIST

The following checklist is used in the Fargo junior high schools.

BEHAVIORAL OBSERVATION AND REFERRAL FORM

Student Name   Grade   Person writing referral   Date   Per.

_____   _____   _____   _____   _____

Attendance

_____ 1. Frequently absent

_____ 2. Frequently tardy

_____ 3. Unexplained gaps of time (e.g., takes 15 minutes to get from one room to another)

_____ 4. Frequently attempts to excuse him/herself from class

Performance

_____ 1. Grades slipping

_____ 2. Assignments late

_____ 3. Assignments poorly done

_____ 4. Not working up to potential/low motivation

_____ 5. Perfect (workaholic)

Attitude

_____ 1. Mood changes from day to day/changes in activity level

_____ 2. Very defensive

_____ 3. Other students are afraid of him/her

_____ 4. Very moody

_____ 5. Hostile or argumentative

_____ 6. Perfectionist (never satisfied with work done even though it's perfect)

Behavior

_____ 1. Disruptive in class

_____ 2. Has changed friends or peer group

_____ 3. Hangs around with students who are associated with chemicals

_____ 4. Family problems

_____ 5. Information associates him/her with chemicals

_____ 6. Vandalism (suspected or actual)

_____ 7. Hangs around lavatories

_____ 8. Thefts or other illegal activity (suspected or actual)

_____ 9. Possession of drug paraphernalia

_____ 10. Frequently at nurse's office

_____ 11. Comes across very sexual with staff member or other students

_____ 12. Doesn't eat lunch

_____ 13. Promises to do better but behavior never changes

_____ 14. Denial of any problem

_____ 15. Avoids contact with concerned persons

_____ 16. Withdrawn, loner

Physical Symptoms

_____ 1. Appears dazed, giddy, or out of it

_____ 2. Falls asleep in class

_____ 3. Appearance is untidy

_____ 4. Changes in facial color and/or degree of alertness from day to day or hour to hour

_____ 5. Glassy, bloodshot eyes, or dark circles around eyes

_____ 6. Very underweight

_____ 7. Gaunt, malnourished appearance

_____ 8. Unexplained bruises

COMMENTS:

_____

SOURCE: Fargo Junior High Schools. Used with the permission of the Fargo Public Schools.

Index